The ACLS Survey of Scholars—Final Report

The ACLS Survey of Scholars

Final Report of Views on Publications, Computers, and Libraries

By Herbert C. Morton and Anne J. Price
With the collaboration of Robert Cameron Mitchell

Office of Scholarly Communication and Technology
American Council of Learned Societies
Washington, D.C.

UNIVERSITY
PRESS OF
AMERICA

Copyright © 1989 by

University Press of America,® Inc.

4720 Boston Way
Lanham, MD 20706

3 Henrietta Street
London WC2E 8LU England

British Cataloging in Publication Information Available

Co-published by arrangement with
The American Council of Learned Societies

Library of Congress Cataloging–in–Publication Data

Morton, Herbert C.
The ACLS survey of scholars : final report of views on publications,
computers, and libraries / by Herbert C. Morton and Anne J. Price ;
with the collaboration of Robert Cameron Mitchell.
    p.   cm.
Includes bibliographical references.
1. Scholarly publishing– –United States. 2. Learning and scholarship–
–Data processing. 3. Research libraries– –United States. 4. Scholars–
–United States– –Attitudes. I. Price, Anne J. II. Mitchell, Robert
Cameron. III. American Council of Learned Societies. IV. Title.
    Z286.S37M69   1988   88–39482 CIP
    070.5'94'0973– –dc19
    ISBN 0–8191–7260–X (alk. paper)
    ISBN 0–8191–7261–8 (pbk. : alk. paper)

All University Press of America books are produced on acid-free paper.
The paper used in this publication meets the minimum requirements of American
National Standard for Information Sciences—Permanence of Paper for Printed Library
Materials, ANSI Z39.48–1984.   ∞

Contents

Preface

I. *Introduction: Finding Out What Scholars Think* 1
The Tradeoff: Why We Did What We Did 3
Reliability of Results 5
Problems of Interpretation 7
The Special Analysis 12

II. *Results of the Survey* 13
The Sample 14
Professional Reading 21
Scholars as Authors 25
Computer Use 33
Library Use on Campus 45
Nonacademic Respondents in Brief 50
Retired Respondents 52
Written Comments by Respondents 54
Concluding Remarks 57

III. *Appendixes* 59
A. Appendix Tables A-1 to A-30 60
B. Technical Appendix, by Robert Cameron Mitchell 86
C. Survey Questionnaire 90

IV. *Special Analysis* 105
Marketing, User Surveys, and the Library in Transition,
by Paul B. Kantor 105
Supplement A. Notes on Library User Studies 119
Supplement B. Results of the Cross-Product Ratio
Analysis 124

List of text tables

1. Where survey respondents work 15
2. Comparison of scholarly climate at four-year
academic institutions 19
3. Career stages of academic respondents 20
4. Subscriptions to scholarly journals 22

5. Readership of selected periodicals   24
6. Authorship patterns, by discipline   25
7. Publication patterns of faculty, by career stage   26
8. Bias in peer review   28
9. Publications activities during career   30
10. Importance of prepublication material received from colleagues   31
11. Scholarly cooperation during career   32
12. Computer use and experience for all respondents   34
13. Adequacy of library collections in colleges and universities   46
14. Availability and use of three library technologies at colleges and universities   47
15. Ranking of sources of material by scholars at colleges and universities   49
16. Professional activities   53

List of figures

1. The growing proportion of women entering academic life in the humanities and social sciences   17
2. How comuters are used   38
3. Effects of computer use   42
4. Percentage of academic respondents using computerized catalogue   48

List of appendix tables

A-1. Response rate for sampled societies

A-2. Weighting of sample: Size of society memberships and number of respondents

A-3. Profile of society members in sample

A-4. Profile of respondents employed at universities and colleges, by discipline

A-5. Comparison of female and male respondents, by discipline and stage of career

A-6. Changes in journal subscriptions

A-7. Readership of selected general periodicals, by discipline and type of institution

A-8. Keeping up with the literature, by discipline, type of institution, and stage of career

A-9. Opinions on value of articles in major journal, by discipline and stage of career

A-10. Estimated number of articles published during career in refereed journals, by discipline and stage of career

A-11. Percentage of respondents who have written for general publications, by discipline and stage of career

A-12. Publication of dissertation, by discipline and stage of career

A-13. Prevalence of bias in peer review

A-14. Perceived frequency of bias in favor of established researchers in a scholarly specialty, by discipline and sex

A-15. Perceived frequency of bias in favor of scholars from prestigious institutions, by discipline and sex

A-16. Perceived frequency of bias in favor of males, by discipline and sex

A-17. Use of computerized catalogues at academic institutions

A-18. Use of computerized data searches at academic institutions

A-19. Training in using library resources at academic institutions

A-20. Quality of library services at academic institutions

A-21. Convenience of library services at academic institutions

A-22. Importance of sources of materials at academic institutions

A-23. Microfiche use at academic institutions

A-24. Computer familiarity, and hardware and software used

A-25. Comparison of computer uses

A-26. Computer access and experience

A-27. Anticipated effect of computers on the intellectual progress of the discipline over the next five years

A-28. Anticipated effect of computers on how the discipline is taught over the next five years

A-29. Professional reading of retired respondents

A-30. Publications reported by retirees and other respondents

Preface

In August 1986 a preliminary report on the ACLS Survey of Scholars was published by the Office of Scholarly Communication and Technology. The Office, which had been established by the American Council of Learned Societies two years earlier, had sought to obtain the views of more than 5,000 humanists and social scientists on a wide range of issues related to their experience as authors and users of scholarly publications, as users of academic libraries, and as users of computer technology in their research and teaching.

The preliminary report appeared as a special issue of *Scholarly Communication,* the quarterly newsletter of the Office. At about the same time the findings were summarized in considerable detail in the *Chronicle of Higher Education.* The survey results were later reported in numerous publications, including the *EDUCOM Bulletin,* which reprinted the entire contents of the newsletter in its Fall/Winter 1987 issues.

This final report presents a revised and expanded discussion of the survey findings, as well as more than thirty additional tables, a new section on the views of retirees, a technical appendix on the survey procedure, and a special analysis of the library data (by Paul B. Kantor). A copy of the complete survey questionnaire is also appended.

The project was a collaborative effort. Herbert C. Morton and Anne J. Price, director and staff associate, respectively, of the Office of Scholarly Communication and Technology, shared responsibility for every phase of the project, from its conception to completion of the final manuscript. I want to add my personal thanks as well as those of the Board of Directors of ACLS to Dr. Morton, who headed the Office throughout its existence and whose leadership and intelligence deserve principal credit for the Office's great success. Robert Cameron Mitchell, professor of geography at Clark University, was primarily responsible for the survey design and supervised its implementation. He also contributed to the draft of the report and prepared the technical appendix.

The questionnaire was developed jointly by the three major contributors and then submitted to an Advisory Committee, which reviewed it and made numerous helpful suggestions. The committee, which also reviewed the first draft of the preliminary report, was comprised of: Audrey Davis, secretary of the History of Science Society; Janet Griffith, senior research sociologist, Research Triangle Institute; Jules LaPidus, president of the Council of Graduate Schools; Thomas Mann, executive director of the American Political Science Association; and Sharon J. Rogers, university librarian, George Washington University. Useful contributions to the questionnaire were also made by other reviewers and the scholars who participated in a pilot test of the questionnaire. Bettina Hagen prepared successive drafts of the report and assisted in managing the flow of work. Melissa Moye assisted in assembling and summarizing the open-ended comments volunteered by about 750 respondents.

We wish to thank the secretaries of the societies that participated in the survey for their cooperation and suggestions. Several members of the advisory board of the Office of Scholarly Communication and Technology also made helpful comments. Action Surveys of Rockville, Md. handled the data processing.

Copies of the questionnaire and the original data tapes have been sent on request to other researchers studying these and related issues. The data tapes continue to be available from the Roper Center, as explained in Appendix B.

The survey was undertaken with the encouragement of John William Ward, late president of the ACLS, who established the Office of Scholarly Communication, and the late R.M. Lumiansky, ACLS president pro tem. During my tenure, the ACLS continued to support the project until its completion. Financing was primarily from the general funds for the office provided by the Andrew W. Mellon Foundation, the National Endowment for the Humanities, and the Rockefeller Foundation.

—Stanley N. Katz, President
American Council of Learned Societies
June 1988

I. Introduction
Finding Out What Scholars Think

The term "scholarly communication" has gained acceptance over the past decade as an umbrella term covering a wide range of issues that rank high on the agenda of scholars in the humanities and social sciences. These issues—which are also of common concern to librarians, publishers, academic administrators and others committed to the advancement of learning—include:

• the refereeing and publication of journals and books, (as well as the use of informal systems for the exchange of ideas and information)

• the development and use of library collections and networks and of other means for assuring access to scholarly material now and for the long run

• the application of new technology to teaching, research, and publishing

• the governmental system of policies and regulations affecting scholarship, such as the funding of higher education and research, copyright, and restrictions on the free flow of information.[1]

What is distinctive about these issues—and about the groups that are especially interested in them—is their interdependence. As pointed out a decade ago in the report of the National Enquiry into Scholarly Communication, scholars and their societies, publishers, librarians, and so on constitute a system in which the actions of each affect the others—and all are influenced by outside funding agencies and changes in technology.[2]

---

1. For a survey of the literature, see Herbert C. Morton, Anne J. Price, and Others, *Writings on Scholarly Communication: An Annotated Bibliography of Books and Articles on Publishing, Libraries, Scholarly Research, and Related Issues.* Lanham, Md: University Press of America, 1988.

2. *Scholarly Communication: The Report of the National Enquiry,* Baltimore: Johns Hopkins University Press, 1979. The project was sponsored by the American Council of Learned Societies.

1

Although scholars are the central figures in the system, surprisingly little has been reported about their major concerns, their work habits, and their attitudes. In an effort to get such information about their views as producers and users of scholarly materials, the Office of Scholarly Communication and Technology designed and conducted its Survey of Scholars in 1985–86.

The first striking fact about the survey was its response rate. To the surprise of almost everyone who had been consulted about the project, about 71 percent of the more than 5,000 scholars who received questionnaires returned them. The questionnaire was 14 pages long, and according to pretests required a half hour to forty minutes to fill out. Yet the scholars were not put off by the task.

To some extent, the high response can be credited to the support of the learned societies that cooperated in the survey and to the procedures that were followed to foster participation. But more important, in our opinion, is the fact that busy scholars would not have taken the trouble to fill out the questionnaire if they had not believed that the questions being asked were important ones and that the information obtained might, in some way, raise their understanding of the scholarly system and possibly open up discussion of troubling questions.

Generally the pattern of responses was similar among the disciplines, but on particular issues it was not unusual for one society to differ markedly from the others—historians on computer use,

---

Sample in brief

Sample size: 5,385

Number of respondents: 3,835

Response rate: 71 percent

Sex: men, 74 percent, women, 26 percent

Race: white, 95 percent, other, 5 percent

Age: Half under age 45 (59% of women, 48% of men)

Holders of Ph.D. degree: 86 percent (92% among academics)

Memberships: over half of the respondents belong to four or
    more learned societies

linguists on the importance of prepublication materials, sociologists on co-authorship, and so on. There were also clear differences between men and women, between established scholars and newer entrants to academic ranks, between scholars at research universities and those at liberal arts colleges.

A preliminary report on the results was published in our newsletter about six months after the survey was completed.[3] In this final report we seek to elaborate on that earlier one. We hope to make clear the major findings and their implications, the limitations of our research, and the opportunities for further research of this type. We think we have made a useful step forward in exploring the views of an important group of scholars and have stimulated further inquiry by others, but we are under no illusions that we have advanced very far. The issues are complicated and difficult to analyze, and survey research is only one of many tools that are needed to explore them. Practical considerations also led us to compromise on some matters. Simply in editing our final draft of the questionnaire, for example, we had to eliminate about a fourth to a third of the questions to keep the form from being too great a burden on the respondent. Moreover, although our pretest had helped to identify many ambiguities in the questionnaire, it had not given us an insight into all of them. Thus although we think our survey results tell a great deal, we think it important to let the reader know the limitations of the work, at least so far as we can identify them.

To suggest the nature of the limitations inherent in our study, three matters are discussed briefly below: why we did what we did, the relative reliability of certain types of responses, and the broader questions of interpretation.

The Tradeoff: Why We Did What We Did

The issues encompassed by the term scholarly communication apply to all fields of learning and scholarly activity—the humanities, the social sciences, the sciences and the professional fields. But to keep our project to manageable size we decided that we would limit our survey to humanists and social scientists, with the hope that if our findings proved to be promising researchers in other areas would draw on our experience to pursue the questions in their own fields.

3. *Scholarly Communication,* Number 5, August 1986.

The problems of sampling forced us to make a similarly pragmatic decision. How should one select a scientifically sound sample of humanists and sociologists for a survey such as ours? Who should be included, academics only or all professionally active humanists and social scientists? Sample design procedures offer a number of options. For example, one that has been used for major academic surveys is a stratified random sample obtained in a two-step process. First, a number of institutions are selected by size, type of curriculum, geographical location and similar criteria, and, second, respondents are chosen at random from the academic departments in institutions identified in step one. Preliminary estimates indicated that this approach, though methodologically sound, would be too costly and time-consuming for our purposes. Morever, the lists from which the samples would be drawn were of questionable reliability.

After exploring this and other possibilities, we decided on a different two-step approach that we thought would reduce costs, get us more information, and lead to a higher response rate. We decided to draw our sample from the membership of several major societies that belong to the American Council of Learned Societies. We selected societies in seven disciplines: classics, history, linguistics, literature, philosophy, political science and sociology. (See Technical Appendix.) These societies are not necessarily representative of the family of forty-five societies constituting the ACLS or all of the disciplines represented in the membership. But they are among the largest and best known ones and are in traditionally important areas of learning.

This decision limited the statistical applicability of our findings to the relevant ACLS constituencies only, leaving open the question of how useful the sample would be as a proxy for humanists and social scientists generally.

What were the offsetting advantages?

1. By drawing our random sample of respondents from the regularly used and updated mailing lists of the societies, we assured ourselves of a very accurate list at a relatively low cost. Only a handful of questionnaires were undeliverable, and only a few had to be discarded for falling outside our sample definition, which excluded graduate students and society members from foreign countries.

2. By drawing our sample from society memberships, we obtained data not only on scholars employed in colleges and universities, but also on those employed elsewhere. As it turned

out, these nonacademics constitute more than one-sixth of the combined memberships of these societies and, in one field, history, they constitute 28 percent of the members. Had we drawn the respondents from a sampling of university departments we would not have obtained any data about these independent scholars, who as the survey showed, remain highly active and productive scholars in their fields. Comparisons of these "academic" and "nonacademic" scholars (as they are called in this report) offer some interesting information about the kinds of employment and activities of highly trained people who did not follow academic careers but who still feel themselves closely tied to their discipline. We were also able to pick up views of scholars employed outside their disciplinary departments (sociologists in business schools, for example).

3. We also obtained limited information about the 4 percent of the members who are retired, many of whom are still active in scholarly pursuits.

4. By drawing our sample from an available listing of scholars in a discipline, we could easily and efficiently obtain a large enough sample in each one (from 450 to 600) to permit comparisons among fields. (When the results of the data by society were combined to obtain totals, they were then weighted to reflect the relative size of the societies.)

Reliability of Results

Not all of the answers can be given the same credence even though they were obtained by the same statistical procedure because not all of the questions could be answered by respondents with the same accuracy. This is obvious perhaps, but it is worth further examination. To illustrate, one can think of a kind of hierarchy of believability.

Some answers can be accepted without reservation because the questions are unambiguous, deal with well known facts, do not call for subjective evaluation, and offer no apparent incentive for dissembling. In this survey, questions falling into this category are mostly of a personal nature, such as questions about sex and age, or about the discipline with which the respondent is affiliated. Even if errors occur, they will be rare and unlikely to affect the statistical result.

Answers are less reliable when they deal with factual matters that may lie outside the respondent's personal experience or on which the respondent may be poorly informed: "Is your library catalog computerized or being computerized?" Some respondents probably don't know but may guess.

Also of somewhat less reliability are answers that depend on the accuracy of recall. For example, the question, "How many journals do you subscribe to?" is likely to draw a more accurate response than the followup questions: "How many others do you read regularly?" and "How much money did you spend last year on books and journals?" The recall problem increases when questions are asked about the number of articles that have been accepted for publication in refereed journals over a professional lifetime. The question is straightforward and the factual answer could be determined, but in a survey setting, without an opportunity for the respondent to check records, the answer depends on some guesswork.

Judgmental questions may raise a different concern. "Are book prices or journal prices rising too fast?" The respondents are not being asked to provide information about objective changes in prices or the relation between price increases for books and for computers or medical care. The question was not intended to get comparative price data. If that were the purpose, it would have been phrased differently. Rather the question was intended to find out what respondents think. (The importance of the distinction between reality and the respondent's perception of it is illustrated below in the discussion of peer review.)

Questions about opinions introduce another factor, which is the objectivity of the phrasing of the question, its neutrality. Closely related is the importance of maintaining an unbiased sequencing of questions. The effects of changes in wording and sequence have been well documented.[4]

We mention these familiar matters here primarily because this report is addressed to the scholarly communication community—scholars, librarians, publishers and so on—not to specialists in survey analysis and methods who regularly deal with such questions.

In short, as in all research methodologies, there are inherent difficulties in survey research, including the familiar problems of sample, design, neutral and unambiguous phrasing of questions, and the accuracy of the respondents' recall. Even under the best

---

4. An extensive literature has emerged, including a comprehensive two-volume study by a panel of the National Research Council. See Charles F. Turner and Elizabeth Martin, editors, *Surveying Subjective Phenomena*. New York: Russell Sage Foundation, 1984.

of circumstances and under the most careful procedures, opinion surveys may turn up results that are of uneven quality and open to second guessing. We believe it is important to lay out these reservations clearly in advance because in reporting our findings we often make statements with seemingly unabashed confidence. Generally, we rely on the readers' understanding of the context to evaluate how to weigh the evidence. What we offer throughout is our best judgment of the evidence, and we think it would be impractical to repeat at each stage of the discourse all the possible caveats. By and large, we avoid drawing inferences about differences in responses that are not statistically warranted.[5]

But it is not only the problem of statistical reliability that concerns us. We are equally concerned with the difficult matters of making proper interpretations of the results.

Problems of Interpretation

What can we infer from the survey findings? What do they mean? Beyond the problems of statistical analysis lie questions of interpretation that arise in putting the quantitative findings into words and into an appropriate context. Before turning to the systematic description of the findings, which are presented in the next chapter, we discuss two issues that illustrate the kinds of problems of interpretation encountered in this study. The two issues, which attracted special attention when the preliminary report was published, are (1) editorial peer review and (2) the adequacy of library collections and other matters where we chose to emphasize what a minority of the respondents answered rather than the majority view.

1. On the fairness of the system by which manuscripts are reviewed for publication, the survey points to widespread dissatisfaction or uneasiness among scholars. About three out of four respondents think the editorial peer review system is biased (frequently biased in the opinion of 50% of all respondents and occasionally biased, in the opinion of 22% of them). About 40 percent think bias is so prevalent in their discipline that it merits reform. These findings are striking, but what are we to make of them?

First, we need to recognize that a finding that scholars believe the systems to be biased does not mean that it is biased in fact.

5. See Technical Appendix. In addition, Paul Kantor's technique of cross-product ratio analysis, set forth in Part IV of this report, provides confirming evidence of the statistical significance of our major findings.

The survey shows "how a sample of scholars in the humanities and social sciences *think* the system is working not the outcome of a study of *how it works,* which is something quite different."[6]

The respondents' perceptions may not be in accord with reality. They may be based on bad personal experience, hearsay from a colleague who believed a manuscript was rejected because of an unfair assessment, or an ill defined distrust. Since publication is an enormously important issue, especially to younger scholars striving for tenure, and since people generally tend to be defensive about their writing, it is not easy for writers to remain dispassionate about publication decisions affecting their manuscripts. Especially in emerging disciplines or controversial areas, a rejection may be interpreted by an author as a decision based on a reviewer's incompetence or unfairness rather than on the manuscript's lack of merit or unsuitability for the journal to which it was submitted. But apart from the natural defensiveness of authors and the speed of transmission of bad experiences, the most important fact is that no one knows how peer review is working, either in specific publications, particular disciplines or over-all. As discussed below, the subject has been neglected.

Second, when one responds that he or she thinks the system is biased, what is the standard against which the system is being judged? All things considered, have scholars a right to expect that the system should be 99 percent fair or that, realistically, an 80 or 90 percent fairness and competence score is the best that can be expected? To expect fully informed and sound judgments by all referees and editors on all manuscripts is hardly realistic. And it is not essential. The availability of alternative publication opportunities generally offers protection against pervasive injustice arising from bias in the system. The question is, therefore, not whether bias exists in the peer review system, but whether it is prevalent and whether it systematically interferes with the free exchange of information and ideas by discriminating against particular subjects, opinions, and classes of authors.

Whatever the situation may be, however, the fact remains that most of the survey respondents don't trust the editorial peer review system. And so long as that distrust persists, the system of peer review remains in jeopardy, and, in turn, so does the integrity of the academic evaluation process. Given the singular

6. Herbert C. Morton, "Survey of scholars revisited: Bias in peer review," *Scholarly Communication,* Number 6, Fall 1986. The rest of the discussion on peer review is largely taken from this article.

importance of editorial peer review in the promotion and tenure of young scholars and in assuring the quality of scholarly publishing generally, its credibility is essential. The survey raises a warning flag that calls attention to the need to explain why dissatisfaction exists, why it is widespread, and what steps should be taken to restore confidence in the system. The survey shows that suspicions of bias appear to be held by scholars in all types of universities and among all the disciplines sampled. Though it is higher among women than among men and is less prevalent among scholars in the top research universities than in other types of institutions, the unease is pervasive, not an occasional outcropping of discontent.

From other sources, we get confirming indicators that all is not well with editorial peer review, though we are struck even more by how little real evidence exists. The most comprehensive study of how peer review is working in journals was presented in an exceptional book by Stephen Lock, editor of the *British Medical Journal,* entitled *A Delicate Balance: Editorial Peer Review in Medicine.*[7]

Lock's book is of great importance for two reasons: It contains a comprehensive canvassing of published work on peer review over the preceding fifteen years and it presents the results of his own case study of the fate of every manuscript submitted to his journal from January 1 to August 1, 1979. Lock's study left him firmly convinced of the value of the peer view process, but also disturbed by the shortcomings he had observed in the way it operates. He was also deeply troubled by how little was known about how peer review was being conducted. This led him to echo an observation by John C. Bailar and Kay Patterson who had written shortly before his book came out that the subject of peer review had been strangely neglected by its champions. They reported that they had been able to find little scientific work on the subject. "It seems to us that there is a paradox here: the arbiters of rigor, quality and innovation in scientific reports submitted for publication do not apply to their own work the standards they use in judging the work of others."[8]

Bailar and Patterson proposed that a comprehensive study of peer review be conducted by a disinterested major national or international group, a suggestion that Lock endorsed. The sugges-

7. Nuffield Provincial Hospitals Trust, 1985. Published in the United States in 1986 by ISI Press, Philadelphia.

8. J.C. Bailar and Kay Patterson, "Journal Peer Review: The Need for a Research Agenda," *New England Journal of Medicine,* (March 7, 1985).

tion was taken up in 1986 by the American Medical Association, which announced it would sponsor a congress on peer review in 1989, based on research papers developed in the interim.[9]

What the ACLS survey findings suggest is that such a conference would be highly desirable in the humanities and social sciences as well.

2. In reporting our preliminary findings, we decided at several points to stress a minority opinion rather than the majority response because we believed it was more instructive. This decision troubled some of our readers, who thought that we were thereby slanting our findings.[10] The matter is worth exploring briefly because we follow the same practice in the final report.

Part 3 of the questionnaire (Appendix C) dealt with library collections and services. Scholars were asked to rate library collections on a 6-point scale: excellent, very good, good, fair, poor, not sure. Generally, scholars gave their libraries high ratings, but there were some interesting differences in their views. For example, one of the questions asked respondents to rate the adequacy of the library's book, journal, reference, and newspaper collections for several purposes—faculty research and teaching needs, and student needs. Not unexpectedly, a majority of scholars gave all collections a favorable rating, and a higher proportion of scholars at research universities said that the collections were adequate for their needs (that is, "good" to "excellent") than did scholars at all other types of institutions. In contrast, more than half of the respondents from colleges said that both journal and book holdings were inadequate for their research needs, (that is, only "fair" or "poor".)

What was most striking, we thought, was the fact that at every type of institution—research universities, Ph.D.-granting and comprehensive universities, and colleges—the lowest rating was given to the adequacy of book collections for research. Relative to other collections, the collection of books for research purposes was invariably the weak spot. Over-all, 45 percent of the respondents indicated that book collections were inadequate for their research needs. The response was markedly different in most of the other categories. Only about 25 percent or less of the respondents found the reference holdings and the book and journal col-

9. Drummond Rennie, "Guarding the Guardians: Editorial Peer Review," *JAMA* (Nov. 7, 1986).

10. See, for example, Ronald H. Epp and JoAn S. Segal, "The ACLS survey and academic library service," *College and Research Library News* (February 1987).

lections for teaching needs and student needs inadequate.

Thus, in Table 11 of the preliminary report we chose to display the number of respondents who rated the various aspects of the collection as "fair" or "poor", rather than the number who gave ratings of "excellent" "very good" or "good". Our reasoning was as follows. Libraries are generally held in high esteem by scholars. User surveys taken by libraries around the country have generally turned up the same answer, that they are doing a good job. The answer is not very helpful to librarians, except for purposes of self-justification. Not only are such surveys not informative, but also they can lead to a dangerous complacency, according to Herbert White, a library school dean, since "They always turn out complimentary and positive, regardless of level of library service provided."[11]

We thought our study would tell more about user attitudes if we went beyond the typical statements of approval and emphasized the areas where scholars are least satisfied. This, we thought, would be more informative and more helpful. The practice is routine. Educators and librarians are campaigning against illiteracy by citing the large minority of adults who are functionally il-literate; they do not emphasize the much larger percentage who read and comprehend.[12] Similarly, in its monthly report on the labor force, the Bureau of Labor Statistics puts the emphasis on the *unemployment rate,* even though well over 90 percent of the labor force has been at work since World War II. As a problem of social policy, it is proportion of people who are out of work and want jobs that is of greater concern. Thus we think we are on sound grounds in continuing to emphasize the minority view where we think it appropriate to do so.

It is worth adding the following comment to the substantive issue at stake on the subject of the quality of library collections. The survey findings showing the relative inadequacy of book col-lections to meet the research needs of scholars were in line with what librarians have been saying for years: that no library, not even the biggest and best research libraries, can be self-sufficient any longer. It is no longer possible for a single institution to keep up with the vast flow of new materials being produced within the scholarly community. Scholars conducting research

11. Herbert S. White, "The Use and Misuse of Library User Studies," *Library Journal* (December 1985), pages 70-71.

12. Herbert C. Morton and Anne J. Price, "Setting the record straight on the Survey of Scholars," *College & Research Library News* (May 1987).

will inevitably have to draw on resources outside their campus. It was in response to this fact that librarians began many years ago to place greater emphasis on resource-sharing by developing bibliographical networks that would enable scholars to search libraries throughout the country for the items they needed. At the same time experiments were undertaken to facilitate electronic delivery of information.

The Special Analysis

Though we took into account data-weighting techniques and matters of statistical significance from the outset, we did not explore the usefulness of introducing more sophisticated statistical analytic procedures. For the final report, we asked Paul Kantor, a consultant who specializes in issues affecting research libraries, to make a special analysis of the library data employing whatever methodology he chose. His results are presented in Part IV.

Kantor points out that most library user studies apply to only one library and include very little about the scholars—and only the scholars who use the library. Thus the ACLS survey, which is nationwide and is not limited to regular library users, offers a unique body of data. To exploit it, Kantor uses the cross-product ratio technique, which he says has advantages of clarity and resistance to bias in analyzing the responses. He generated about 600 "interesting correlations," several hundred of which are statistically significant, and selects a few for discussion. His presentation focuses as much on demonstrating the potential for deriving further useful inferences from the survey data and for encouraging further research as on offering additional specific substantive conclusions. He also points out that one of the contributions of the survey was the development of a questionnaire that can serve as a standard instrument which an individual library can use to obtain information about user attitudes toward its collection and services. The results can then be compared with those of the national survey.

II. Results of the Survey

Some results of the ACLS Survey of Scholars confirm what is generally known; others help identify or clarify new issues. A few illustrative findings, in addition to those mentioned in the introduction, suggest the nature and scope of the survey.

• *The rapid increase in computer use.* In 1980, about 2 percent of all respondents either owned a computer or had one on loan for their exclusive use. In 1985, the number was 45 percent, most of whom used it not only for routine wordprocessing but for other purposes as well. (Some special applications are taking hold slowly. For example, only 7 percent of the respondents report having sent a manuscript to a publisher in machine-readable form.)

• *Informal communication.* More than 20 percent of all respondents consider prepublication distribution of articles by their colleagues to be at least as important to them as articles read in journals.

• *Favoritism.* Three out of four respondents consider the peer review system for journals in their discipline biased, especially in favor of established scholars. Nearly half say reform is needed.

• *Library use.* The interlibrary loan is regarded as of "great" or "moderate" importance by 51 percent of scholars at colleges and universities; 19 percent attached the same importance to computerized database searches. These are two of the services that are essential for coping with the library problem most frequently identified by academic respondents: the inadequacy of their campus library for meeting their research needs.

• *Effects of computers.* Asked whether they thought the long-run effect of computers on research in their disciplines would be "very positive, positive, neutral, negative, very negative or don't know", computer users in colleges and universities were overwhelmingly positive while half of nonusers were undecided. Only 4 percent of users and 8 percent of nonusers thought effects would be negative.

• *Authorship.* Slightly over half of the academics said they had published their doctoral dissertation either as a book or, in part, as a journal article; three out of four have published at least one article in a refereed journal.

This report includes data on all respondents, on academics alone, and on nonacademics, as appropriate. The sections on professional reading and scholars as authors emphasize data on all respondents while the sections on computer use and libraries are focused on the academic respondents at colleges and universities.

The Sample

The ACLS survey is based on a stratified random sampling of 5,385 scholars in colleges and universities and working outside the academic community. Usable questionnaires were returned by 3,835 of those surveyed, a response rate of 71 pecent.

The sample was obtained in a two-step process. First, we selected ACLS societies in seven disciplines—classics, history, linguistics, English and American literature, philosophy, political science and sociology—that are illustrative of both humanistic and social science approaches. Second, we selected society members at random (excluding foreign members and graduate students). Our response rate was sufficiently high and our sample size was sufficiently large to allow us to generalize to society memberships with considerable confidence. We must add, however, that those who responded are not necessarily representative of the highly diverse ACLS membership, of their disciplines, or of the humanities or social sciences generally. They do, nonetheless, represent a large, highly productive, and influential segment of the scholarly community whose activities tell us a good deal about the state of scholarship today.

The sample of historians was selected from the domestic membership lists of two societies, the American Historical Association (10,850) and the Organization of American Historians (5,612). In literature, the sample was selected from a group of 9,100 members of the large Modern Language Association (27,000) who teach English or American literature. Other disciplines are represented by sampling, in each field, the domestic membership of a single society: classics: American Philological Association, (1,950); linguistics: Linguistic Society of America (2,100); philosophy: American Philosophical Association (5,500); political science: American Political Science Association, (5,500); sociology: American Sociological Association, (9,000).

For convenience in exposition in this report, the name of the discipline is frequently used instead of the society name, but the results are properly applicable only to the society. Where the data for the societies are combined, figures are weighted to reflect the relative sizes of the society memberships.

Characteristics of respondents

Colleges and universities employ 78 percent of the members of the societies sampled, including administrators with faculty status (5%) and those who hold nonfaculty administrative or research positions (3%). About 18 percent of the respondents are employed outside academe, but the percentage varies widely by field, ranging from 10 percent of the respondents in literature to 28 percent in history. About 4 percent of the respondents are retired. (See table 1).

Table 1. Where survey respondents work

(Percentage of society members in academic and nonacademic jobs)

| Place of work | Discipline of participating societies | | | | | | | |
	All	Literature	Classics	Philosophy	History	Linguistics	Political Science	Sociology
College or university	**78**	**85**	**75**	**88**	**67**	**82**	**81**	**73**
Faculty member	70	78	72	84	58	75	74	62
Administrator with faculty status	5	5	2	3	6	3	5	5
Nonfaculty	3	2	1	1	3	4	2	6
Nonacademic	**18**	**10**	**17**	**11**	**28**	**17**	**15**	**23**
Industry, nonprofit, government	7	2	3	3	9	10	7	13
Other[a]	11	8	14	8	19	7	8	10
Retired	**4**	**5**	**8**	**—**	**6**	**1**	**4**	**4**
Total, all respondents	100	100	100	100	100	100	100	100
Size of sample (N)	*3835*	*636*	*451*	*481*	*611*	*493*	*575*	*588*

Percentages may not add to 100 because of rounding

[a]Secondary schools and self-employed primarily

A higher proportion of academic respondents work full time (94%) than nonacademics (80%). Only 2 percent of the academics are employed less than half time.

Although membership in the societies is open to all scholars, those who belong are likely to be self-selected from the most trained and most active persons in the field. Thus 92 percent of the academic portion of the sample (and 62 percent of the non-academics) hold the Ph.D. Half of all survey respondents belong to four or more professional societies; only 8 percent belong to one.

There are clear (though not surprising) differences in demographic patterns among societies. For example, in linguistics and literature, the percentage of all respondents who are women is much higher (36% and 38%, respectively) than the average of 26 percent; it is lowest in political science (15%). The level of nonwhite membership is highest in linguistics (10%) most of whom are Asian-American. Political scientists report the highest levels of family income (which includes income earned by the respondent's spouse). Next in line are the historians and the sociologists, who do much more consulting. (Almost twice as many earn more than $1,000 a year from consulting compared to the average of other respondents.)

The academic profile

Most academic survey respondents are tenured faculty members and a relatively high proportion of them are full professors. (For a summary profile of academic survey respondents see appendix table A-4.) About two out of three respondents said they had tenure, which is in line with estimates by Bowen and Schuster, as well as others, for tenure in higher education generally.[1] Four out of ten have the rank of full professor, whereas surveys of faculty across the board traditionally show a fairly even split among the four ranks, professor, associate professor, assistant professor, and instructor and others.[2]

One of the most marked changes in the academic profile over the past few decades is the increase in the percentage of women (see figure 1). This trend is clearly reflected in the survey data for faculty by career stage shown in appendix table A-5. Among respondents who began teaching before 1965, only 8 percent are women; 92 percent of this cohort was male. Over the ensuing years the proportion of women rose steadily. For the 1980–85

[1]Howard R. Bowen and Jack H. Schuster, *American Professors: A National Resource Imperiled.* New York: Oxford University Press, 1986. The authors report that tenure is higher at public institutions, 68.1%, than at private ones, 55.7%, but has risen in all types of institutions during the past two decades. They caution, however, that because of disparities in data from different sources, the evidence is sometimes difficult to assess. See table 3-7, page 45.

[2]Bowen and Schuster, *American Professors,* page 44. In recent years the proportion in the top ranks has increased slightly.

Figure 1. The growing proportion of women entering academic life in the humanities and social sciences
(Percentage of men and women at different career stages in 1985)

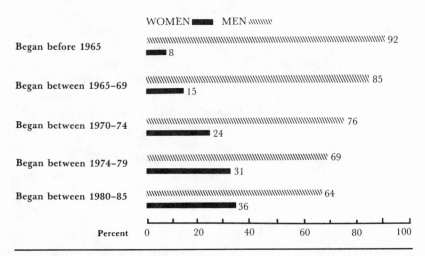

WOMEN ▬▬▬   MEN ∖∖∖∖∖∖∖

Began before 1965   92
8

Began between 1965–69   85
15

Began between 1970–74   76
24

Began between 1974–79   69
31

Began between 1980–85   64
36

Percent   0   20   40   60   80   100

career group, the proportion of women is 36 percent. Overall, the survey shows that women account for 25 percent of the academic respondents.[3] The average age of women academics is 43.7 years; men averaged 46.4 years.

Among the disciplines represented in the survey, linguistics had the highest proportion of respondents with the Ph.D., 96 percent. In higher education generally, the increase in the percentage of faculty with the Ph.D. has also been substantial since World War II, rising from 38 percent of full time faculty in 1947–48 to 70 percent in 1980; an additional 10 percent had the M.D. or other professional degree. By that time the percentage with a bachelors degree "diminished almost to the vanishing point."[4]

The Carnegie Commission on Higher Education has classified institutions of higher learning into five categories: (1) research universities that award at least 50 Ph.D.s a year, (2) Ph.D.-

[3]Bowen and Schuster estimate that the percentage of full-time faculty members who are women has risen from 16.9 percent in 1960–61 to 27 percent in 1980–81; the growth in the percentage of women getting the PhD has been even more dramatic, from 13.3 percent of all degrees awarded in 1969–70 to 36.9 percent of those awarded in 1984–85. See *American Professors* pages 57 and 58.

[4]Bowen and Schuster, *American Professors,* p.33.

granting universities that award between 10 and 49 Ph.D.s a year, (3) comprehensive colleges or universities that offer a liberal arts program as well as one or more other degree programs such as teacher training or engineering which enroll a significant number of students, (4) liberal arts colleges that primarily grant liberal arts degrees, and (5) two-year colleges and institutes. All but 6 percent of our academic scholars teach at four-year institutions: 39 percent at research universities, 14 percent at Ph.D.-granting universities, 23 percent at comprehensive institutions, and 17 percent at liberal arts colleges. In our final tabulations we combined categories 2 and 3 since we found no discernible differences between scholars in Ph.D.-granting universities and those at comprehensive colleges and universities.

The nature of the institution and the department in which scholars teach affect their teaching load, the type of students they have in their classes, and the pressures on them to publish. These two factors are also related to productivity and, to a lesser extent, to job satisfaction. About 44 percent of the respondents teach in departments that offer the doctorate, and another 22 percent teach in departments that offer a masters but not a doctors degree. Asked about their mix of graduate and undergraduate teaching responsibilities, three out of four respondents said they teach mostly or all undergraduates, but among those who teach at research universities, the percentage is much lower (47%). Among those in Ph.D.-granting departments who describe their department as among the top ten departments in their discipline (26 percent of the sample made this claim), just one of four faculty members reported teaching mostly undergraduates.

Teaching loads are inversely related to the emphasis placed on research by the scholars' institution. Table 2 shows the mean annual course loads as reported by respondents. At research universities, the load averages about two courses per semester; at other schools, three courses or more a semester is the norm.

Scholars were asked to rate the pressures to publish scholarly articles and books at their institutions on a five-point scale from extremely strong to very weak. More than half of those at research universities report extremely strong pressures, a level of expectation that drops sharply for the other types of schools. Only 4 percent of those teaching at liberal arts colleges report extremely strong pressures to publish.

Responses to a question that asked: "Overall, how satisfied are you with your current job as a college teacher or administrator?'' showed that three out of four respondents are either very satisfied or mildly satisfied. Less than one in ten are very unsatisfied. Although those teaching at research universities report somewhat higher levels of satisfaction than those at other types of institutions, the factor that appears to affect satisfaction the most is the perceived quality of the scholar's institution. Fifty-nine percent of those who say their school is extremely selective in admitting undergraduates and 66 percent who rate their department as among the top ten in their discipline say they are very satisfied with their jobs.

Table 2. Comparison of scholarly climate at four-year academic institutions[a]

(Academic respondents)

Category	Research university	Ph.D. university, comprehensive college or university	Liberal arts college
Annual mean teaching load			
Semester courses	4.2	6.0	6.4
Quarter courses	5.1	7.1	7.5
Pressure to publish			
Extremely strong	52	14	4
Strong	34	34	20
Moderate or less	14	53	76
Total	100%	100%	100%
Job satisfaction			
Very satisfied	47	38	41
Mildly satisfied	33	34	32
Neutral or unsatisfied	19	28	27
Total	100%	100%	100%

Percentages may not add to 100 because of rounding.

[a]The classification of institutions used in this survey is based on definitions published by the Carnegie Council on Policy Studies in Higher Education.

Of particular importance for comparing the disciplines on the various items in the survey is the finding that there are distinct differences in the type of university or college where members of the disciplinary societies teach. Linguists are twice as likely to be found in research universities (64%) than scholars in the fields of literature (36%), history (33%), and philosophy (32%). Compared to those in the social science disciplines, there is a greater tendency for those in the humanist disciplines of literature, philosophy and history to work in institutions they rate as not very selective in admitting undergraduates. Classicists differ from their fellow humanists (and the other disciplines as well) in that they are more likely to find employment in private institutions (54%) and to work in institutions that are "most selective" in admitting undergraduates (36%).

In the analysis that follows, significant differences between the disciplinary samples show up primarily in the areas of scholarship and publishing where the scholars' work setting is likely to facilitate or hinder these activities. Thus the fact that linguists are the most likely of all the scholars to report having published an article in a refereed journal may be attributable in part to the fact that more of them work in settings where publishing is facilitated by lower teaching loads and greater rewards.

Another significant feature of the academic profile by discipline is the proportion of respondents at different career stages. Historians are relatively older, linguists and sociologists younger. As shown in table 3, a much higher proportion of historians began their teaching careers before 1965 (31% compared to an average of 22% for all societies). In linguistics and sociology, on the other hand, a much smaller proportion entered teaching before 1965, and a higher percentage (26% and 27%) began their careers in the 1980–85 period. Comparisons between respondents in early and late career stages are made frequently throughout this report and show clear, though not unexpected, contrasts in reading and authorship patterns, computer use, and so on.

Table 3. Career stages of academic respondents

(Percentage in each cohort group, by discipline)

Start of teaching career	All	Literature	Classics	Philosophy	History	Linguistics	Political Science	Sociology
Before 1965	22%	19%	26%	22%	31%	17%	23%	16%
1965–1969	16	18	13	18	17	19	13	13
1970–1974	17	19	19	18	13	17	17	20
1975–1979	20	20	19	17	19	22	22	24
1980–1985	24	24	23	26	20	26	25	27
Total	100	100	100	100	100	100	100	100

Percentages may not add to 100 because of rounding

Professional Reading

Spending by all respondents for books and journals averaged about $450 in 1985, according to the estimates reported on questionnaires. Scholars spent twice as much for books ($300) as for journals ($150), including journals received as part of society memberships. (The total is equal to about 1.4 percent of the published estimates of average salary of faculty of all ranks in 1984-85.) Spending for books was highest among classicists, a fourth of whom estimated that they spent more than $500.

Scholars on campus spent nearly 40 percent more for books than other scholars; book expenditures tended to be higher at research universities and among scholars who mainly teach graduate students. Spending for journals varied, ranging from under $100 for 29 percent of the respondents to more than $300 for 12 percent of the respondents.

Journals

One of the laments of many editors of humanities journals is that circulation is stagnant or dwindling because scholars are relying more on library copies and reducing their own subscriptions.

There is no evidence from the survey to support this generalization, though it may be true for some scholars and particular journals. Indeed, the evidence seems to point the other way. Two-thirds of all academic respondents (and four out of five of the scholars who have been teaching more than twenty years) report that they received the same number of scholarly journals in 1985 as they received the preceeding year (table 4). As for the others, more said they increased the number of their subscriptions than decreased them. (19 percent compared to 13 percent). This pattern was rather consistent across disciplines, although classicists made fewer changes and sociologists somewhat more subscription cutbacks than the others. There was little difference between university scholars and nonacademics, or between those teaching in colleges and those in research universities. The most striking contrast was that between scholars in the late and early stages of their careers. About 78 percent who began teaching before 1965 maintained the same number of subscriptions, compared to 58 percent of those who began teaching in 1980 or later. On the other hand, 30 percent of the younger group said they increased the number of their subscriptions.

Among those who said they decreased the number of subscriptions, the reason most frequently cited was the need to cut ex-

Table 4. Subscriptions to scholarly journals
(Number of current subscriptions and percentage of respondents
making changes)

Discipline or stage of career	Average number of journals	Changes in number from previous year		
		No change	Increased	Decreased
All respondents	**4.7**	**67%**	**19%**	**13%**
Literature	4.6	65	22	13
Classics	4.4	76	14	10
Philosophy	3.7	69	16	12
History	4.7	72	15	12
Linguistics	5.1	64	23	13
Political Science	4.8	65	22	13
Sociology	5.2	62	21	17
Academic respondents only	**4.8**	**67**	**20**	**13**
Began teaching before 1965	5.1	78	10	11
Began teaching in 1980 or later	4.3	58	30	11

Note: About 1 percent of the respondents do not subscribe to any journals.
Percentages may not add to 100 because of rounding

penses (41%). The other major reasons given were the lack of time to read (30%), change in field of interest (10%), and the increase in subscription rate (5%).

Among scholars who said they were employed in the top graduate departments of their discipline, the lack of time was cited as frequently as the desire to cut expenses.

Overall, scholars appear to satisfy their principal journal needs largely by subscription, buying more than they read regularly in the library. Sixty percent of the respondents say they subscribe to four or more journals, three of which are included in society memberships. Less than 10 percent subscribe to only one journal. At the other extreme, 10 percent subscribe to nine or more. Scholars outside colleges and universities appear to subscribe to almost as many journals as those on campuses.

In the college and university community, the number of subscriptions is greater (1) among scholars at research universities than among those at colleges, (2) among scholars in mid or late career, and (3) among those who teach mainly graduate students.

Respondents were also asked how many other journals they monitor systematically. Of those who answered, one third said none, and almost half said they examine three or more journals regularly as soon as they come out, in addition to the four or five they subscribed to. There was little difference among scholars in different disciplines, except for classicists who tend to browse more widely and sociologists who follow fewer journals. About 90 percent of respondents said they also occasionally (at least once a year) look at additional journals (some peruse more than ten).

The average number of journals read by all respondents and by scholars in different disciplines appears below.

	Copies by subscription	Copies examined regularly
All respondents	4.7	3.7
Literature	4.6	3.6
Classics	4.4	6.7
Philosophy	3.7	3.9
History	4.7	3.9
Linguistics	5.1	3.5
Political Science	4.8	3.7
Sociology	5.2	2.8

In sum, it appears that the average respondent follows about a dozen journals: four or five by subscription, three or four more that are monitored regularly, and four or five that are occasionally checked.

Other periodicals

In this era of increasing specialization, questions have been raised about the proportion of scholars who read general interest periodicals edited to reach a broad cross-section of scholars and others. To obtain a preliminary indication, the survey asked scholars if they read a variety of other periodicals ranging from national book review publications to science magazines. Their responses indicate that book review publications (*The New York Times Book Review, Times Literary Supplement* and the *New York Review of Books*) enjoy the widest readership. They are read "regularly" by half of the respondents and "occasionally" by nearly 32 percent more. (See table 5). The *Chronicle of Higher Education* is read regularly by 24 percent of the respondents (73 percent of the academic administrators). Readership of scientific periodicals is higher among linguists, philosophers and sociologists, and it is higher among nonacademics than academics.

Table 5. *Readership of selected periodicals*

(Percentage of all respondents reading selected periodicals outside their discipline during past year)

Periodical	Total	Read regularly	Read occasion- ally	Read once	Not read
Book review publications[a]	100	50	32	4	13
Chronicle of Higher Education	100	24	38	10	28
Science periodicals[b]	100	16	27	10	47
American Scholar	100	5	16	9	71

Percentages may not add to 100 because of rounding

[a]*New York Times Book Review, Times Literary Supplement, New York Review of Books*

[b]*Science, Scientific American, Technology Today, Science 85*

Book buying

Scholars report that they buy about twenty-one books a year for their personal libraries, including 12 paperbacks, at a cost of more than $300. Social scientists buy fewer; historians and philosophers, classicists and literary scholars buy more. Scholars who are not affiliated with universities buy fewer books than academic respondents (in contrast to their purchases of journals, which was about average).

There is a strong consensus among respondents on scholarly book prices: Four out of five agree or strongly agree that most scholarly books are "very overpriced" even after taking inflation into account; only 2 percent have no opinion!

Readers' concerns

Keeping up with the literature in their field seems equally troublesome to scholars on campus and off. Scholars were asked to respond to a very strong statement: "It is virtually impossible to even minimally keep up with the literature in my field." Most scholars chose "strongly agree" or "agree", but the response varied. Those who teach at research universities report slightly lower levels of frustration than those teaching in colleges, and keeping up seems easiest for respondents in the classics and most difficult for those in literature. Younger scholars generally say keeping up is less difficult.

Another strong statement asked respondents their views about their discipline's major journal. One out of ten strongly agreed that "I rarely find an article that interests me" when "I look at a new issue'' and another 23 percent agreed. A majority disagreed (55%). The percentage of scholars who rarely find an article of interest was highest in the social science disciplines of political science (43%) and sociology (41%) and lowest in linguistics (19%).

On the responsiveness of the book reviewing process, nearly half of the respondents express dissatisfaction, though few of them feel strongly about the matter; 46 percent think that books are not reviewed fast enough, 29 percent think they are, and 26 percent haven't made up their mind. A majority of political scientists and linguists find the reviewing process too slow; literary scholars are the least dissatisfied. Respondents who teach mostly graduate students also indicate considerable impatience.

Scholars as Authors

The most common mode of publication is the journal article: 73 percent of all survey respondents say they have had at least one article published in a refereed journal. (See table 6.) Among

Table 6. Authorship patterns, by discipline
(Percentage of all respondents who are authors or co-authors of types of publications)

Discipline	Type of publication				
	Article in refereed journal	Book[a]	Chapter	Book review in scholarly journal	Short story, novel, poetry
All fields	**73**	**45**	**52**	**66**	**13**
Literature	74	40	48	65	30
Classics	75	46	38	66	13
Philosophy	76	39	49	64	9
History	66	52	47	72	7
Linguistics	81	45	56	63	13
Political science	73	51	63	64	6
Sociology	78	41	60	61	8
Academic	**78**	**47**	**56**	**70**	**13**
Nonacademic	**53**	**30**	**37**	**43**	**11**

[a]Except textbook; 17% of respondents said they had written or were co-authors of a textbook (25% in linguistics and political science)

Note on authorship of other types of publication by all respondents:
Comment in refereed journal: 27%
Book review in newspaper or magazine: 27%
Scholarly paper in conference proceeding: 59%
Nonfiction essay, article in newspaper or magazine: 39% (political science, 51%)

academics, it is 78 percent—which is the same percentage reported in the 1984 Carnegie survey. A third have published five or more articles; 7 percent report 20 or more.

Publication patterns seem to vary only slightly by discipline, as shown in table 6. Historians and political scientists are more likely than the others to write scholarly books; linguists are more likely to write articles. Literary scholars are more likely than others to turn to novels, stories, and poetry but for most modes of publication they are closest to the average, followed by classicists and philosophers.

Scholars in academic institutions publish substantially more work than scholars in other employments, generally about 50 percent higher than for nonacademics. (For example, 78 percent of academics have published an article, compared to 53 percent of those employed in government, business, and so on.) An exception is conference proceedings, where the difference between the two groups is much less. The difference is even greater when the number of articles is compared. The median number for academics is 6.0 compared to 2.6 for the others.

Publication patterns differ among respondents at different stages of their career. In the academic community, for example, scholars concentrate on journal articles early in their careers; half of them also write book reviews and conference papers. Over time, more of them write a variety of other works, including scholarly books. As shown in table 7, most respondents who

Table 7. Publication patterns of faculty, by career stage
(Percentage of scholars at universities and colleges who have published at least one of the various types of publications)

Type of manuscript	Academic respondents	Began career	
		1980 or later	Before 1965
Article in refereed journal	78	70	88
Scholarly book review	69	50	89
Paper in conference proceedings	63	48	74
Chapter in scholarly book	55	38	76
Scholarly book (author)	47	23	73
Scholarly book (editor)	29	11	50
Comment in a refereed journal	29	14	44
Newspaper or magazine article	38	30	50
Book review in popular publication	28	19	50
Textbook	19	6	37
Short story, novel, poetry	13	13	14

began their teaching careers before 1965 report they have written publications in five or more categories. (But even about 12 percent of these respondents have not had a journal article published.) These established scholars have published an average of 9.6 articles, compared to an average of 2.7 for scholars who began their careers in 1980. It appears that the growth in the number and variety of publications continues into late career.

Articles that are published are generally accepted by the first journal to which they are submitted. Three out of four academic respondents said their most recent publication appeared in the journal to which it was originally sent; about 9 percent said they sent their manuscript to three or more journals before acceptance.

Pressures to publish are reported to be strong or very strong by most academic respondents, but weak or very weak by most of the nonacademics. Within the academic community, differences follow along expected lines by type of institution, as discussed earlier.

Scholars were also asked whether all or part of their dissertation had been published in the original or revised form (excluding the microform copy). Most indicated that it had been published in some form, as noted below:

	All respondents
All or most published as book or monograph	22%
Part in a book or article	33
None of it	36
Did not write a dissertation	9

At research universities, three out of four of the respondents published at least part of their dissertation in some form.

Attitudes on peer review and publishing opportunities

The survey reflects considerable dissatisfaction with the peer review system, notwithstanding efforts by many editors in recent years to adopt procedures aimed at improving the fairness of the system. Three out of four respondents consider peer review biased in favor of certain groups of scholars; nearly half say the system is defective enough to require reform. In colleges and universities women are more critical than men, and younger scholars (teaching since 1980) are much more critical of peer review than are scholars who began teaching before 1965.

The question on peer review read, "How often, if at all, do you think the peer review refereeing system for scholarly journals in your field is biased in favor of..." As shown in table 8, half of all the scholars said the system is frequently biased in favor of established researchers and those who use "currently fashionable approaches." Another 22 percent said this happens "occasionally." Those who believe these groups are not favored are very few, indeed: 5 percent said 'infrequently" and 4 "rarely or never" (19 percent said they were not sure). Those who feel that holding a position at a leading university frequently gives the

Table 8. Bias in peer review

(Percentage of respondents reporting frequent and occasional favoritism toward specific groups by journals in their discipline)

Favored group	Bias "occasional" All respondents	Bias "frequent"				
			All respondents		Academics	Scholars in top graduate schools[a]
		Total	Low and high disciplines	Female	Male	
Established researchers	22	50[b]	43 history 56 sociology	63	47	44
Scholars in prestigious institutions	24	42	32 linguistics 46 sociology	51	38	27
Scholars using "currently fashionable" approaches	22	50	33 classics 56 sociology	59	49	49
Males	11	13	9 linguistics, political science 16 sociology, literature	32	7	8

[a]Self-selected. Respondents who say they are employed in one of the top ten graduate departments in their discipline.

[b]An additional 5 percent of the respondents think bias occurs infrequently, 4 percent said bias was rare or never occurred and 19 percent weren't sure. See appendix table A-13.

person an edge with the referees total 41 percent. Only 13 percent believe bias in favor of males is frequent.

Although women at colleges and universities think the peer review system favors men, they believe sex bias is much less prevalent than other forms of bias. Forty nine percent believe that men are frequently or occasionally favored whereas a much larger group—80 percent of the female respondents—think established scholars are favored frequently or occasionally, and 71 percent think scholars in prestigious institutions are favored.

Male respondents generally think bias of any type is less of a problem than female respondents consider it to be.

The number of academics who feel "the peer review system in my discipline needs reform" is 42 percent.

Opinions are divided on the question of whether tenure committees should consider refereed material published in nontraditional forms (microform, electronic journals and so on). A plurality (41%) favors the broader definition of publication, but almost as many are neutral or have no opinion; 21 percent are opposed. Among linguists, philosophers and classicists, however, half favor acceptance of nontraditional publications.

By a substantial majority, respondents believe that there are enough journals and book publishers in their field, but probably enough of them disagree to suggest that new publishing ventures will continue to be started. One in six respondents thinks more journals are needed, (but only 3 percent feel strongly about the matter) and one in five thinks more book publishers are needed. Among sociologists and classicists, one in four want more book publishers in their fields, and almost as many sociologists want more journals. Length of teaching career and other factors seem to have little effect in shaping these views.

Although several learned societies have issued information to help their members decide where to send their articles (modern language, sociological, political science, and philosophical associations) one respondent in five thinks additional information is needed. Responses are clearly related to length of teaching career: 30 percent of those who started teaching in 1980 or later want help, compared to 12 percent of those who began teaching before 1965.

Only a small minority of respondents—about 7 percent—have as yet submitted a book or article manuscript to a publisher in machine-readable form.

Refereeing and editorship

Scholars serve not only as researchers and writers but also as evaluators—determining what is worth publishing and suggesting ways to improve the quality of scholarly publications. Well over half of the survey respondents have served as journal referees or editors.

Scholars are much more likely to serve as referees of journal articles or to evaluate a book manuscript for a publisher if they teach at research universities or are well established (see table 9). Whereas 56 percent of all respondents say they have refereed a journal article, 79 percent of those in research universities have been referees. There is some variation among disciplines, with participation in the review process more widespread among political scientists and sociologists. A much higher proportion of

Table 9. Publications activities during career
(Percentage of respondents in different roles)

Group or discipline	Journal referee	Journal editor	Reviewer of book manuscript
All respondents	**56**	**24**	**52**
Literature	48	24	44
Classics	56	19	48
Philosophy	54	24	54
History	48	19	50
Linguistics	63	31	54
Political science	68	19	61
Sociology	67	31	57
Nonacademic respondents	**34**	**17**	**30**
Academic respondents	**61**	**25**	**57**
Research university	79	35	73
Liberal arts college	44	15	40
Stage of career			
Began before 1965	76	34	79
Began in 1965–69	76	31	73
Began in 1970–74	69	29	66
Began in 1975–79	65	25	56
Began in 1980 or later	44	15	32

scholars who began teaching before 1965 have served as referees —76 percent compared to 44 percent of scholars who began in 1980 or later. Responses on the number who have evaluated book manuscripts for publishers are similar.

About a fourth of all respondents have served as journal editors. Relatively more respondents in linguistics and sociology have been editors.

When data on these three editorial and peer review activities are combined, they show two out of three respondents have participated in at least one of these activities.

Collaboration

There has been much discussion in recent years about "invisible colleges," the growing importance of the dissemination of pre-publication material, and related evidence of informal exchanges of ideas. More than two thirds of the respondents receive material from colleagues before it is published, but the percentage is lower among scholars in literature and classics.

The survey shows that one respondent in five reports that prepublication material from colleagues is at least as important as material read in journals. (A very small fraction consider it more important. See table 10). Differences among disciplines are very

Table 10. Importance of prepublication material received from colleagues

(Percentage of all respondents, by discipline)

Discipline or institution	Total	More important than journals	As important as journals	Useful but less important	Of little or no importance	Do not receive
All respondents	100	4	17	29	19	31
Literature	100	2	11	26	19	43
Classics	100	3	15	26	18	39
Philosophy	100	5	16	30	21	28
History	100	4	12	29	21	35
Linguistics	100	11	34	26	12	17
Political science	100	5	19	31	23	22
Sociology	100	5	24	33	16	22
Nonacademic	100	6	15	22	13	43
Academic	100	4	17	31	20	28
Those at: Research university	100	6	25	35	17	16
Liberal arts college	100	3	15	28	16	39

Percentages may not add to 100 because of rounding.

pronounced. About 45 percent of the linguists consider this literature as important or more important than journal articles, compared to only 13 percent of scholars in literature. An additional 26 percent in linguistics find pre-publication materials useful, though less important than journal articles. Women in colleges and universities tend to accord somewhat higher importance to pre-publication material than do men.

To what extent do scholars consult with or collaborate with colleagues at their institution or elsewhere? Answers to questions related to this issue provide a useful perspective on informal scholarly communication. Although such communication is the general rule, it is far from universal.

About a fourth of all respondents report that no one in their department or present organization shares any of their research interests. The percentage is higher among scholars employed outside universities and colleges than among academics. Even in research universities, one scholar in ten finds no one with similar research interests. The number is 7 percent among scholars who say they are in the top 10 percent of the graduate department in their discipline. Classicists and historians tend to find themselves more isolated than scholars in other fields. There is no difference between men and women on this issue.

Scholars at colleges and universities find fewer colleagues with whom to share their results. About 40 percent have no one in their departments to ask for comments on their manuscripts; in research universities the percentage is almost 30 percent (see table 11).

Table 11. Scholarly cooperation during career
(Percentages of scholars in colleges and universities)

Category	Ever co-authored paper or publication with colleagues		At present one or more people in your department	
	In department	Outside department	Share your research interests	Regularly comment on your work
All academics	**25**	**42**	**77**	**61**
Sociology	52	69	83	70
Linguistics	34	60	80	66
Political Science	33	55	78	64
History	15	28	69	53
Philosophy	16	30	75	63
Literature	14	22	80	55
Classics	10	27	70	55
Research universities	33	52	89	71
Liberal arts colleges	14	32	62	59

For all respondents, co-authorship is more frequent among scholars who work at different places. About 40 percent of the academic respondents have been co-authors with outside scholars, compared to 25 percent within their institution. Disciplinary differences in co-authorship emerge clearly. Half the academic sociologists have been co-authors with department colleagues whereas only a tenth of the classicists have done so. Collaborative authorship among linguists, political scientists and especially sociologists is much higher than among other scholars.

Use of electronic mail or networks to facilitate collaboration is still very rare. Overall, only about 4 percent say they have tried it for that purpose, though among linguistics scholars and sociologists, the figure is 10 percent. A slightly higher percentage have distributed a paper by electronic means.

Computer Use

The survey shows a high level of computer use among all respondents. More than 90 percent have access to a computer, over 50 percent report that they or their research assistants routinely use a computer of some kind. Forty-five percent now own or have exclusive use of a personal computer that they use in their work. (Table 12 summarizes data on computer use for all respondents).

In the following discussion, computer use among scholars at colleges and universities and among those working outside of academic settings will be covered separately. The pattern of use is similar for all respondents, but the exposition will be clearer and more precise if each group is treated alone.

Scholars at colleges and universities

One fourth of the 3,002 survey respondents working in academic settings report they have access to a dedicated word-processing system, 39 percent to a minicomputer such as a VAX, 58 percent to a mainframe computer, and 77 percent to a microcomputer (personal computer). Access differs only slightly for scholars at different types of four-year schools except for access to mainframe computers, which is much higher for those who teach at research universities (67%) and lower for those at liberal arts colleges (50%).

And scholars are using these computers: over 50 percent of those on campus routinely use computers in their writing, research, or teaching, and another 19 percent are occasional users. There are differences among the disciplines, but they are not large. Historians use computers least (44% report routine

Table 12. Computer use and experience for all respondents
(Percentages)

	All respondents							
	All	Literature	Classics	Philosophy	History	Linguistics	Political Science	Sociology
Access to a computer *N = 3835*								
Yes	93	93	93	94	90	96	94	95
No	7	7	7	6	10	4	6	5
Routinely use a computer[a]	51	49	47	54	41	56	53	58
Occasionally use	18	15	15	16	17	23	19	26
Do not use	31	36	38	30	42	21	28	16
Have computer for exclusive use	45	46	41	50	37	59	46	50
Use at home	29	34	27	33	26	38	27	26
Use at office	7	6	6	8	6	8	8	11
Use both places	9	6	8	9	5	13	11	13
Touch typing skill fair to excellent	86	87	82	86	87	89	84	85
Word processing skill fair to excellent	61	59	58	64	52	74	62	69
Computer programming skill fair to excellent	22	10	16	19	12	33	27	42
Place of nearest computer *N = 3143*								
In own office	34	27	31	27	31	42	36	44
In nearby office	37	37	36	40	37	33	39	37
Elsewhere	28	37	33	34	32	25	24	20
Had experience with computers in graduate school *N = 3682*	25	8	8	9	14	25	40	58
Have written a computer program								
for research *N = 2855*	14	5	9	6	7	28	18	30
for teaching *N = 2793*	9	5	12	11	3	15	12	14

[a]Including use by assistant

use) while sociologists, linguists, and philosophers report the most routine use (61%, 57%, and 57%, respectively, slightly higher than the figures for these disciplines in Table 12, which shows totals for all respondents).

Computer access and use on campus

Most respondents at colleges and universities say they have access to mainframe computers and microcomputers; some have access to minicomputers; however, those with access are more apt to use self-contained micro- or personal computers than any other type, as shown below.

	Percent with access	Percent of those with access who use
Microcomputer (PC)	77	62
Mainframe central computer	58	27
Minicomputer serving multiple users	39	19
Wordprocessing system	25	17

Sociologists, political scientists and linguists use mainframe computers far more than other scholars, and more linguists and sociologists use minicomputers than scholars in other disciplines.

Most academics who use computers have easy access to them: 31 percent use computers (or terminals) in their own offices and 39 percent use computers in nearby offices. Sociologists and linguists are more likely to have computers in their offices, as are scholars in research universities, and those at the leading graduate departments. A very large majority (70%) of those who use computers report that the machines are available to them all or most of the time.

Among respondents working at colleges and universities, 50 percent own computers or have them on loan for their exclusive use. Although most of these respondents have purchased computers, the survey put both "own" and "on loan" categories together since the key factor is availability not ownership. Many academic institutions provide computers to faculty members on long-term loan or by other special arrangements, to be used on campus or at home. Since the terms of these arrangements may make it difficult for faculty members to answer "yes" or "no" to a question on whether they own a computer, the question was phrased "Do you personally own (or have on loan for your exclusive personal use) a personal (micro) computer or computer terminal which you use for your work either at home or at your institution?"

The rise of personal computers on campus has occurred over a period of about five years although the technology was introduced nearly a decade ago. The first Apple II personal computer was released in 1977. By 1980 only 1 percent of college and university respondents had a personal computer. A year later when IBM began selling its personal computer, 3 percent had personal computers. Growth in personal computer acquisition grew exponentially in the next three years so that by 1984, one in three on-campus respondents had personal computers; by late 1985 the proportion had risen to half. The cumulative percentage of academic based scholars who have their own personal computers is as follows:

Year	Cumulative percentage
1980 or earlier	1%
1981	3
1982	7
1983	16
1984	32
1985 (10 months)	50

Most respondents who use computers do their own computer work. Seventy-three percent do all or most of their own word processing, text and data management, communication, etc., ranging from 80 percent of linguists to 66 percent of sociologists and historians.

Factors relating to computer use

Most campus-based respondents have the basic skills that are necessary to use a computer, but relatively few are prepared for programming: 64 percent rate themselves as "excellent" or "good" at touch typing (22% rate themselves "fair") and about half are "good" or "excellent" at wordprocessing. Only 21 percent have at least a "fair" ability to program computers; however, in sociology, 41 percent say they are at least "fair" at programming computers.

The length of time a scholar has been teaching is related to routine computer use. Scholars who began teaching before 1970 are less likely to be using a computer than those who began their careers later.

Began teaching	Percent who use computers
Before 1970	45%
1970–1979	56
1980–1985	64

Younger scholars are also more likely to have used computers in graduate school. about a third of those who began teaching in 1980 or later had at least a "fair" amount of experience with computers in graduate school compared to 4 percent of those who began teaching before 1970. This percentage will be larger in the future as about half of the survey respondents report that their institutions are "strongly" or "very strongly" encouraging undergraduates to use computers.

How computers are used

Respondents are not using computers just as enhanced typewriters for simple wordprocessing, but are taking advantage of the computer's ability to search and sort large amounts of text as well as numerical data. Respondents were asked to rate 16 uses for a computer on a five point scale from "very important" to "very unimportant." The combined ratings of "very important" and "somewhat important" are reported in figure 2. Five uses stand out. Wordprocessing leads the other uses; 95 percent of users rate it as very or somewhat important. The others in order are, maintaining note files, preparing tests, compiling an index or bibliography, and statistical analysis.

There are significant differences in the way computers are used by different disciplines, in part, due to the types of analysis appropriate for a discipline's subject matter. Linguists tend to list a large number of functions as important or very important for their work than do users in other disciplines. Compared with the other disciplines, historians list fewer functions as important to them.

Almost one in five respondents rate use of the computer to gain access to an institution's online library catalogue as important. This function was especially important to literary scholars. More respondents at research universities listed this function as important than those at liberal arts colleges.

Almost one in five computer users rates computer access to online service networks, including bibliographic databases, as important. The proportion is higher among political scientists and sociologists. Considerably more scholars at liberal arts colleges rate this an important use than those at other institutions. (As noted in the library section, 41 percent of academic respondents have actually used online services, but a very large majority of these have had librarians do their searches.)

Outside of linguistics, only one respondent in ten thinks the computer is important for communicating with colleagues inside or outside the institution. More scholars at research universities rate this function as important than those at liberal arts colleges.

Almost one fourth of those using computers rank computer graphics as an important function, but among sociologists the percentage is much higher (37%).

Fewer than one in five scholars views computer-aided instruction as an important use of computers. Responses vary by discipline—from history, where 8 percent consider it important, to political science and sociology where the percentages are 22 and

Figure 2.   How computers are used
Percentage of computer users at colleges and universities who rate each application as very important or somewhat important

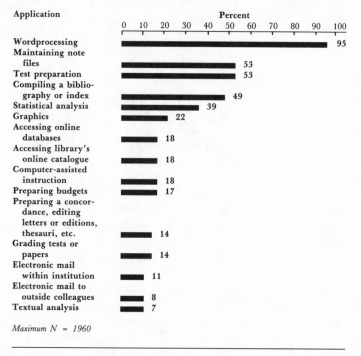

Application	Percent
Wordprocessing	95
Maintaining note files	53
Test preparation	53
Compiling a bibliography or index	49
Statistical analysis	39
Graphics	22
Accessing online databases	18
Accessing library's online catalogue	18
Computer-assisted instruction	18
Preparing budgets	17
Preparing a concordance, editing letters or editions, thesauri, etc.	14
Grading tests or papers	14
Electronic mail within institution	11
Electronic mail to outside colleagues	8
Textual analysis	7

Maximum N = 1960

28 respectively. Scholars at liberal arts colleges think it more important than those at research universities. Finally, few scholars use the computer for only one function. Most use it for several. Over a third rated five to seven functions important, and 31 percent rated three or more important.

Respondents were asked whether they approached their disciplines from the perspective of the humanities, the perspective of the social sciences or each about equally. It is when respondents are grouped by these categories that the strongest difference in computer use is found. Self-reported social scientists indicate greater use of computers than self-reported humanists.

Nearly 60 percent of social scientists say they use a computer in their research and teaching compared with 49 percent of the humanists. Those who say they use both approaches about equally report a level of computer use between the two extremes, 56 percent.

This difference is largely due to the social scientists' use of computers for statistical analysis. Social scientists have been routinely using mainframe computers for statistical analysis for twenty years or more and many of them first used computers as graduate students. Six of ten social scientists say they used computers at least a little in graduate school compared to only one in ten humanists. Over 40 percent say their skill in the use of statistical packages such as SPSS is excellent or good compared with 1 percent of the humanists and 10 percent of those who use both approaches.

While social scientists had a head start in using computer technology, the availability of personal computers and of a variety of software in the past few years has made computers increasingly important to humanists as well. When computer users were asked which computer functions were important to them, with the exception of statistical analysis and graphics, there was little difference between humanists and social scientists in either the range of functions listed or the percentage rating the functions as important or very important.

Scholars with their own computers

Among those who use computers routinely, about seven out of ten have their own computers and, of these, 65 percent use their computers at home rather than at their offices; one in six use them in both places.

Asked the make of their current computer, 40 percent report that they have an IBM (28%) or IBM-compatible machine (12%); 13 percent have an Osborne or Kaypro, 9 percent a Macintosh, and 10 percent an Apple IIe. Classicists were significantly above the average in their ownership of Macintosh computers, which was one of the first computers with the graphics capability to display classical alphabets.

Scholars who have their own computers have purchased a wide variety of software programs for their machines. Eighty-five percent own one of the standard word processing programs. Thirty-nine percent have purchased data or file management programs (over 50% of sociologists). Twenty-one percent have purchased a data management and word processing program designed specifically for scholars such as Nota Bene, while 19 percent own a program with multiple capabilities such as Lotus 1-2-3. Statistical analysis and spreadsheet programs are more common among political scientists and sociologists.

About 30 percent of those who have their own computers have modems, which is in line with the number who use their computers for accessing databases and communicating with other scholars. Far more linguists, political scientists, and, especially, sociologists have modems than other scholars.

The questionnaire asked scholars why they obtained their first computers. By far the majority said they obtained computers to help with their writing. Next in importance was assistance in research activities and in teaching (each was cited as an important factor by over 20 percent of those with computers of their own or on loan).

A large majority (81%) of computer users say they are very satisfied or satisfied with their wordprocessing software. They also report a high level of satisfaction with the software they use for statistical analysis, database management, grading and recordkeeping, and, to a lesser extent, teaching. However, an average of one in five scholars—almost one in three of the linguistic scholars and classicists—has a software need that is not being met by software manufacturers. These needs are discussed below in the review of written comments by respondents.

Few computer users at colleges and universities have written programs for computers: 10 percent have written programs for classes and 13 percent for their research (24% for their research in linguistics and 26% in sociology).

Problems

Scholars were asked to list their most common problems in using computers. A third said they had none. The most frequent answers given by those who had a problem were insufficient access to a terminal and the lack of advice and assistance in using the computer, each mentioned by one in six. A sixth of the classicists and linguists report they have problems in getting software to do what they want to do.

Incompatibility between computers continues to present difficulties. Although 39 percent of computer users are able to transfer the work from their own computers to their institution's computer system and vice versa, another 18 percent can only do this with difficulty, and 28 percent report the systems are totally incompatible. (The remainder do not know whether they can do this or not.)

Effects

One of the most controversial issues in the advent of computers into nonscientific research has been whether their use would have a negative effect on scholarly research, over-emphasizing its quantitative aspects. The questionnaire asked scholars whether computers will have a positive, negative, or neutral effect on the intellectual progress of their discipline in the next five years. Computer users are much more optimistic than nonusers, as shown by the comparisons below; three of four users are positive whereas half of the nonusers haven't made up their minds. But in both groups the number who think the effect will be negative is less than 10 percent.

	Computer users	Nonusers
Very positive	23%	5%
Positive	49	36
Neutral	20	35
Negative	3	6
Very negative	1	2
Don't know	4	15

There is little difference between the disciplines: philosophers tend to be more neutral and linguists the least negative. Less than 10 percent of respondents in any discipline are negative.

The questionnaire asked respondents to predict the effect of computers on how their discipline will be taught to undergraduate and graduate students over the next five years. Optimism about positive effects is considerably less on this score. Only two of five predict a positive effect. In linguistics, political science, and sociology, however, nearly half or more predict a positive effect. Again, the fear of negative effects was very small: only 6 percent of respondents feel the effect would be negative.

A substantial number of respondents who use computers report that computers have improved their work in a number of ways. The questionnaire asked scholars to rate the effect of computers on such things as their writing efficiency, research productivity, and research creativity on a seven point scale ranging from greatly improved to greatly impaired. Respondents gave the highest rating to an improvement in their writing efficiency: three out of four reported their efficiency was greatly improved or improved. Only 13 percent said computers had little or no ef-

Figure 3.   Effects of computer use

(Percentage of academic respondents who report that using a computer has improved or greatly improved their work*. Center vertical line shows the average for all societies. The range is shown by vertical lines to the left and right. Lowest and highest ranking societies are indicated.)

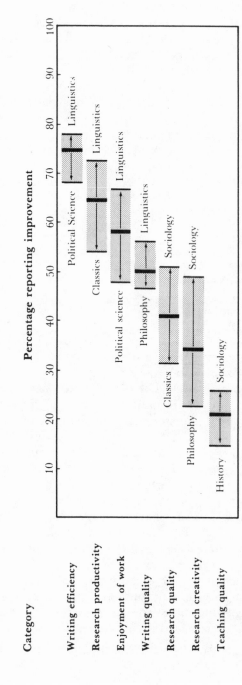

Percentage reporting improvement

Category
Writing efficiency
Research productivity
Enjoyment of work
Writing quality
Research quality
Research creativity
Teaching quality

* Scale was: greatly improved, improved, slightly improved, little or no effect, slightly impaired, impaired, greatly impaired. One percent each said that the quality of their writing and their enjoyment of their work as a scholar was "slightly impaired"

fect on their writing efficiency and here, as in other aspects of their work, only one percent said it had a negative effect. More than half report much improvement in their research productivity. Interestingly, the positive effects reported are not limited to efficiency. More than half say using computers has improved their enjoyment of their work as a scholar (one in four say this is greatly improved), half claim that the *quality* of their writing is improved, and 41 percent make the same claim about the overall quality of their research. More modest, but still substantial, is the number of computer users at colleges and universities who report improvement in their research creativity and the quality of their teaching. (See figure 3.)

The effects vary by discipline. Computers make it possible to explore large data sets in new ways and sociologists, who report much greater reliance on statistical analysis, have the highest percent who credit computers with improving their research creativity and the quality of their research. In linguistics, a discipline with an unusually high number of scholars teaching at the graduate level, the highest percentage of respondents report improvement on a number of dimensions from writing efficiency to writing quality. Wordprocessing and the textual analysis capabilities of computers probably lie behind the finding that literary scholars rank second among those whose enjoyment of their work has been improved by computers.

As shown in figure 3, differences among the disciplines are rather narrow on the questions of writing efficiency and writing quality (falling within a 10-point range) and much wider on questions of research quality and research creativity (about 25 points).

Nonusers

Of those who do not now use a computer even occasionally (about 25% of respondents), over 40 percent said they planned to do so either in the 1985–86 academic year or in the near future. The survey did not ask whether this is because computers are becoming available to them or because they have decided computers would be valuable in their work.

Scholars who are not using computers were given a list of possible reasons and asked to indicate which best describes why they have not yet done so. Almost half said they did not feel it would be of any use to them or that computers were more trouble than they were worth. Only one in ten nonusers answered that they feel intimidated by computers, but the proportion was higher among literary scholars and historians.

Scholars working outside academic settings

In all but a few respects, computer users who work outside a college or university are very similar to those working inside. Forty-nine percent are routine computer users and another 20 percent occasional users. Overall they have somewhat less access to computers (87% versus 96%) particularly to mainframe and minicomputers. However, they use wordprocessors more often than do scholars at academic institutions.

Outside scholars fell into two groups in their use of personal computers, those who have trouble gaining access to a computer and those with unlimited access. Many do not have access at all and only 42 percent have a computer of their own, compared to 48 percent of college and university scholars. Outside scholars who do have access to personal computers are more likely to have computers in their offices and be able to use them at any time. Computer use by outside scholars and academics is compared below.

	Academics	*Nonacademics*
Have computer for exclusive use	48%	42%
Use at home	32	24
Use at office	8	7
Use both places	8	11
Computer programming skill fair to excellent	21	33
Had at least some experience with computers in graduate school	23	34
Have written a computer program		
for research	13	25
for teaching	10	9

Off-campus respondents make slightly more use of computers for online service networks and electronic mail than respondents in colleges and universities. Other functions listed as more important by off-campus computer users were: preparing concordances, dictionaries, critical editions, or editions of letters; preparing budgets; statistical analysis of data; and using computer graphics to prepare charts and diagrams. They list about the same number of computer functions as important as scholars on campus.

In general, off-campus respondents have had more experience with computers than those on campus; a larger percentage have had at least a little experience with computers in graduate school, have written a computer program for their research (25% compared to 13%), and list their general interest in computers as one of their reasons for obtaining a computer. Significantly more feel that computers have improved or greatly improved their creativity in examining their research data in new ways.

Library Use on Campus

Almost all of the respondents have access to a library. Even those working outside colleges and universities report they can obtain from a library within their institution or elsewhere at least some of the scholarly materials they need. This section will deal exclusively with libraries in the academic setting since it is much more difficult to generalize about facilities off campus. The summary profile of respondents not affiliated with colleges or universities in the next section includes a few comments on library use.

Collections and service

How well are research and teaching needs being met by libraries at universities and colleges? The response of scholars to library collections and services is mixed. When asked to rate the adequacy of their library's book and journal holdings for: (1) their specialized research needs, (2) their teaching preparation needs, and (3) their student's needs, a majority of academic respondents generally gave favorable ratings, but many also indicated areas of dissatisfaction (ratings of "fair" or "poor").

As shown in table 13, the scholars' research needs are the needs that are least well served at all types of institutions, but there is much less dissatisfaction with collections at research universities. On each of the categories listed in the table, the percentage of respondents who give ratings of "fair" or "poor" is roughly half as high at research universities as it is for the other institutions.

A higher proportion of newer academic scholars—those who received their Ph.D. in 1980 or later—find shortcomings in their institution's library. They are less satisfied than those who received their Ph.D.'s in the early 1970s or before, in part, perhaps, because after receiving their Ph.D.'s from research universities they began their teaching careers at less well endowed schools. Dissatisfaction with some collections may reflect the special needs of a field. Thus 43 percent of the historians say newspaper holdings are "fair" or "poor", which is far above the average.

In contrast to the dissatisfaction with some book and journal collections, there was widespread satisfaction with the quality of

Table 13. *Adequacy of library collections in colleges and universities*
(Percentage of respondents rating collections as "fair" or "poor")[a]

Collection type	All	Research University	Comprehensive	Ph.D.-granting	College	Began teaching 1980-1985	Before 1965
Book holdings for my research needs	45	26	55	57		53	31
Journal holdings for my research needs	35	18	45	52		45	22
Newspaper holdings	29	17	34	37		29	24
Book holdings for my teaching needs	24	14	30	29		33	12
Reference holdings	22	12	29	27		30	13
Book holdings for my students' needs	21	14	27	26		30	12
Journal holdings for my teaching needs	21	11	25	28		29	8
Journal holdings for my students' needs	18	11	23	25		26	10

[a]The question: "Please give your personal rating of your institution's library..." Choices were "excellent", "very good", "good", "fair", "poor", "not sure".

library service. The scholars were asked how often they were unnecessarily inconvenienced by long lines, malfunctioning equipment, or the inability to get help from librarians. "Seldom" or "very seldom" was the response given by three quarters or more of them.

Satisfaction with the adequacy of interlibrary loan service was also high at all types of institutions (see appendix table A-20), but considerable dissatisfaction with access to computerized data bases was expressed by scholars outside research universities.

Evaluation of technologies

Particular attention was given to scholar's use of and satisfaction with three library technologies: microfiche, online data bases, and computerized card catalogues. Microfiche is a relatively long established medium, and experience with it is widespread. Three out of four academic scholars say they have used microfiche at least once or twice in their careers. Availability of microfiche readers at their institution's library is almost universal (88%), but only 75 percent of the respondents say their library has microfiche materials in its collection which they have used or might want to use. Those who had actually used microfiche in the last three years (68%) were asked to say how satisfied they were with its readability, ease of use, availability, and ability to make satisfactory paper copies. As shown in table 14, satisfaction was reasonably high with all but the quality of paper copies.

Table 14. Availability and use of three library technologies at colleges and universities

(Percentage of academic respondents)

Technology		Avail-able [a]	Have used
Microfiche		88%	76%
Readability of fiche satisfactory	64% of users		
Access to machines adequate	74% of users		
Quality of paper copies satisfactory	25% of users		
Computerized data base searches		80	41
Results of recent searches very			
or midly satisfactory	65% of users		
Computerized catalogues		45	29
Increased access to scholarly materials[b]	38% of users		
Made use of the library more enjoyable[b]	37% of users		
Increased productivity as a researcher[b]	23% of users		
Increased productivity as a teacher[b]	17% of users		
Maximum N = 2944			

[a]"Yes" or "probably yes". Two categories in a 5-point scale.

[b]"Significantly" or "moderately". An additional 15–25% said computerized catalogues had "a little" positive effect in these areas.

The other two library technologies are computer-based. The first is computerized searches of online data bases such as ERIC, MLA Bibliography, and Sociological Abstracts. Availability of computerized searches on campus seems to be almost as widespread as microfiche but use is much lower. About half as many scholars report having every used this technology (41%) as have used microfiche (76%).

Half or more of all academics who have used computer searches reported that most of their costs have been paid by the library, department or institution. About a fifth said, "I paid." At research universities 17 percent said they charged most of their searches to grants (compared to 5 percent at other institutions). Fourteen percent of sociologists and linguists charged most of their searches to grants, but in other fields grants were far less important sources of funds.

About three out of four faculty respondents say that their searches are performed by a librarian, with the scholar present over half the time. Classicists, however, are somewhat more likely to conduct the search without assistance. Satisfaction with the results is fairly widespread. Most respondents say they are "very satisfied" (22%) or "mildly satisfied" (49%).

The other electronic technology is the computerized card catalogue. This is the most recent of the three technologies to be introduced on campus and, according to our respondents, the least available. Forty-seven percent of academic respondents report that part or all of their library's catalogue is currently accessible by using a computer terminal—65 percent at research university libraries and 21 percent at college libraries. About two-thirds of those who have a computerized card catalogue available to them report having used it. These users were asked to rate its effect on several aspects of their work. About one out of three say it has "significantly" or "moderately" increased their access to scholarly materials. Twenty percent say it has increased their productivity as a researcher and 15 percent their productivity as a teacher. When asked whether it has made their use of the library more enjoyable, 32 percent of the users indicated that it had. Figure 4 puts these findings in a different perspective by showing use and improvement as a percentage of all academic respondents.

At this relatively early stage in the scholar's use of library computing, it appears that a very large majority of survey respondents have access to computerized data searches and about half are served by libraries whose catalogue is computerized at

Figure 4. Percentage of academic respondents using computerized library catalogue

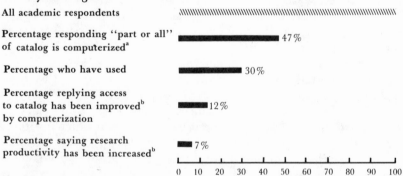

All academic respondents

Percentage responding "part or all" of catalog is computerized[a]   47%

Percentage who have used   30%

Percentage replying access to catalog has been improved[b] by computerization   12%

Percentage saying research productivity has been increased[b]   7%

0   10   20   30   40   50   60   70   80   90   100

[a]Including 6% who say catalog "probably is computerized"
[b]"Moderately" or "significantly" improved or increased

least in part. In both cases, use is much lower than availability even when, as is the case with computerized card catalogues, no charge is imposed for use in the library. Two out of three users are at least mildly satisfied with the results of their computer searches. Only one in three of those who have used computerized card catalogues report increased access to scholarly material. The social scientists are slightly more likely to report these effects than are the humanists.

Ranking of sources

The respondents were asked to rate the importance to them—for "keeping up in your field, your teaching, or your research" —of six sources of scholarly materials, such as books and journals. Scholarly materials already in their personal library are of "great importance" to the greatest number of scholars, as shown in table 15. Materials in the scholars' institution's library rank third after the scholars' recent book and journal purchases.

Table 15. Ranking of sources of material by scholars at colleges and universities[a]

(Percentage of respondents rating sources as of "great importance")

	All disciplines	Discipline with highest percentage		Research university	College
Materials in personal library	77	Philosophy	84	81	73
Materials I purchased during past year	62	Philosophy	71	65	61
Materials in my institution's library	48	Classics	63	59	39
Interlibrary loan	28	Classics	42	23	33
Colleagues' copies	7	Linguistics	16	8	4
Identified through computer literature search	6	Sociology	12	6	8

[a]Question: "Listed below are various types of scholarly materials which you may or may not have used—read, browsed, copied, etc.—during the past year for *keeping up in your field, your teaching, or your research*. Please rate the importance to you of each of the following sources of such materials. (Do not include textbooks in answering this question.)"

Answer choices: "Great importance, moderate importance, slight importance, no importance, did not use"

Material received through interlibrary loan is of great importance to 28 percent of academic respondents. Even at research universities it is almost as high. At colleges the figure is much higher. An additional 24 percent of academic respondents consider interlibrary loans "moderately" important.

Importance of the different sources varies among disciplines, Philosophers, for example, were the most likely to rely on materials in their personal library. Whether they were employed at research universities or at colleges, they still depended most on their personal library.

Briefing users

How much of an effort is being made to acquaint faculty with new library technologies and services? When respondents were asked whether workshops or seminars were provided at their institution to acquaint them with the new services available at the library, nearly half (46%) said "no." At research universities, however, two-thirds of the respondents said that such opportunities were provided. They were also asked whether their institution provided orientation or instruction programs. Three out of four said that such a program was provided for freshmen, (86% at colleges), but only 37 percent said it was provided for juniors and seniors and 40 percent for graduate students. A slightly higher proportion of respondents were not sure whether guidance on use of the library was provided or not. In some fields, about half of the faculty said they did not know whether their graduate students were getting any help on library use.

Nonacademic Respondents in Brief

About one in six of the active scholars who responded to the questionnaire (662 out of 3,835) are employed in government, business, nonprofit institutions and secondary schools, or are self-employed. The percentage varies by discipline, from 10 percent in literature to 23 percent in sociology and 28 percent in history. In response to a question asking respondents to indicate their discipline, 17 percent of the nonacademics describe their field as "interdisciplinary" or "other." The interdisciplinary designation is more frequently given by respondents in literature, linguistics and sociology than by respondents in other fields.

The extent to which nonacademics share the interests and activities of the campus scholars varies from question to question. Differences rather than similarities are emphasized in the recapitulation below, but this emphasis should not obscure the fact that nonacademics who maintain memberships in learned societies retain a strong attachment to their disciplines. They read a little less widely and write fewer articles but they are active in their societies, express similar views on many academic issues and are making similar uses of new computer technology. (Data on nonacademics are included in most of the appendix tables.)

Reading and writing

Nonacademic respondents spend less money on journals and books than academics. A larger proportion of them subscribe to only one or two journals, and they tend to buy fewer books than academics.

The nonacademic respondent is less likely to be the author of a scholarly publication: 38 percent of them have never submitted an article to a refereed journal, compared to 16 percent of the academics. Nevertheless, their contribution to scholarly literature is significant: 53 percent have published an article in a refereed journal, 37 percent a chapter in a book, and 30 percent have been the author of co-author of a scholarly book.

Scholars outside the campus are about half as likely as academics to have served as a referee for a journal or reviewer for a book publisher and are also less likely to have served as a journal editor. They are much less likely to have received a research grant of $1,000 or more. They are less likely to find co-workers in their organization who share their research interests, and fewer ask their colleagues to comment on their draft manuscripts. Nevertheless, about one in four has been the co-author of a paper with a colleague, the same as the percentage among academics.

Although relatively fewer receive pre-publication material, those that do accord it as high importance as academics.

About 95 percent of the academics have written a Ph.D. dissertation but fewer than 75 percent of the nonacademics have done so, and relatively fewer of them published any part of the dissertation.

Nonacademics belong to fewer societies: More than half belong to one to three societies, whereas more than half of the academic respondents belong to four or more.

Although nonacademics also tend to be less active in society activities (serving on a committee or giving a paper) about 75 percent of them have attended a professional meeting in the past three years.

They share the prevailing view on the shortcomings of peer review, and a slightly higher proportion seem to think the peer review system in their discipline needs reform.

Computer use

Computer users outside the academic community make slightly more use of online networks and electronic mail than users on campus. They are more likely to have database or file management programs and to make greater use of a variety of computer functions, including graphics. A higher proportion of nonacademics have written a research program for a computer. Nonacademics report more difficulty than academics with incompatibility between their own and their institutions' computers.

Library use

Slightly fewer of the nonacademics have access to libraries, but those that do rate the journal and book collections and library services as excellent for their purposes. They are as likely as the academics to make computer searches of the literature, and when they do so they tend to rely less on librarians and more on themselves. They make less use of interlibrary loans, and in comparison to their own collections and other sources, tend to find the library slightly less important to their work. The frequently heard complaint about the difficulty that outsiders have in gaining access to research libraries does not show up statistically, but it is reflected in the written comments appended to some questionnaires.

Retired Respondents

Approximately 4 percent of the survey's respondents are retired. While small, the group is not unimportant. It is composed of scholars who are active in their societies, who keep up with the literature, and who have published very extensively.

Three societies equally account for almost 70 percent of retirees: classics, history, and literature. Sociology and political science account for most of the remainder; only 4 percent are from linguistics and 1 percent from philosophy. As might be expected of an earlier generation of scholars, retirees are more frequently male and are less likely to have a doctorate than other respondents. The findings reported below are for all retirees who responded, a total of 158. This group is too small to be broken down into subgroups for analysis, but it can be compared as a whole with academic and nonacademic respondents.

The retirees are almost as active as nonretired academic respondents, in playing leadership roles in their society. As shown in table 16, 70 percent have attended a meeting of their professional society in the last three years, 34 percent have given a paper there, 39 percent participated on a panel, 30 percent chaired or served on a professional society committee, and 20 percent served as a society officer. The retired members gave fewer papers or panel presentations than active nonretired members but served about as often on committees or as officers.

Table 16. *Professional activities*

(Percentage of retirees and other respondents active in professional societies within the past three years.)

Activity	Retired	Academic	Nonacademic
Attended a professional society meeting	70%	93%	75%
Gave a paper at a society meeting	34	70	41
Participated on a society panel	39	56	34
Chaired or served on a society committee	30	37	22
Served as an officer	20	23	14

The retired respondents report that they keep up with publications in their scholarly fields. They subscribe to fewer journals than nonretired academic respondents, but still read an average of 6-7 journals regularly and periodically scan additional ones. (See appendix table A-29). They bought slightly over half as many scholarly books in the past year as academic respondents.

The retired scholars in the survey have impressive publication records. All say they have edited a book and have written at least one scholarly book or monograph, chapter in a scholarly book, and an article and a comment in a refereed journal (appendix table A-30). Thirty-nine percent have written at least one textbook. Since the high numbers reflect total career publications, they are not truly comparable with those of scholars who are still employed. Nevertheless the retired scholars who stay active in their societies are clearly those who have been among the most productive, as shown below where their publication record is compared with that of academic respondents who began their careers before 1965:

	Retirees	*Scholars who began before 1965*
Wrote a scholarly book	100%	72%
Edited book	100	49
Wrote textbook	39	37

Those who are retired say they are more satisfied with the number of journal outlets in their fields than those respondents still working in the academic community; 84 percent feel the number of outlets are sufficient versus only 71 percent of nonretired academic scholars. They are slightly less critical of the peer review system, about 30 percent agreeing it needs reform in comparison with about 40 percent of nonretired academics.

Retired scholars have taken to computers almost as enthusiastically as nonretired scholars. Thirty-six percent of retired respondents own their own computers as do 50 percent of nonretired academics and 42 percent of nonacademics. While retired respondents list wordprocessing as their most important computer use, they also use computers for statistical analysis and compiling bibliographies and indexes. Markedly fewer retired respondents (50%) than nonretired academics (67%) and nonacademics (64%) are familiar with computerized searches of online databases. And relatively more retired respondents are reserving judgment about the probable effects of computers on the intellectual progress of their disciplines. Forty-seven percent feel the computer's effect will be positive and 27 percent are unsure, while 64 percent of nonretired academics feel the effect will be positive and only 7 percent are unsure.

Scholars who choose to stay active in their professional societies after retirement appear to be primarily those who have been among the most active and productive during their careers. They may be expected to become an increasingly important factor in the scholarly community as the number of older people in our society increases substantially and the large post World War II cohort of academics reaches retirement age. The scholars in this group have been very productive during their careers and, though retired, continue to read widely in their scholarly fields and remain active in their societies. In the future such retired but still active scholars may well represent a new and important perspective in scholarly research and communication and a major force in the professional societies.

Written Comments by Respondents

Survey respondents were encouraged to comment on the areas covered in the questionnaire and to list any computer software they needed but could not obtain. Of those completing the questionnaire, about 750 (or almost 20 percent) included written comments covering a wide variety of topics, and 409 responded with their software needs. The comments are difficult to analyze since they cover a wide variety of topics, with each topic discussed by only a few respondents. However, they provide an insight into some of the respondents' views about their scholarly environment that is not reflected in the survey statistics alone.

Pressures and problems

One in four of those who commented were critical of the scholarly environment in which they work. The pressure on scholars to publish was criticized by many. One respondent noted "there is pressure to publish, though there is virtually no interest in content...the single most important academic achievement one can have is the awarding of a grant." Others wished that the criteria for awarding tenure would include credit for development of computer methods or publication of textbooks.

Close to 175 respondents commented on various aspects of computer technology from the lack of computer training opportunities to the effect of computers on their scholarly profession. Many respondents mentioned the negative aspects of the new technology and warned that while computers may increase research quantity, they do not necessarily increase quality. One wrote, "the profound changes that will result from growing computerization must not be confused with intellectual progress...an advance in productivity perhaps, a change of style, a reorganization, etc., but not necessarily the precursor of an advance in thinking or true progress for the discipline." A political scientist wrote "Reliance on hard data is costing political science a sense of what politics is all about because it is devaluing the units of analysis. It's a problem for all of the social sciences...and it is resulting in elegant models which mean nothing in the overall scheme of intellectual and social development."

While more than half of the users of computerized catalogues reported that computerization increased their access to scholarly materials, some commented that the computerized systems were difficult to use. Others added that computerized bibliographical searches need to be supplemented by reference to the printed card catalogue, since "the information obtained is dependent on the judgment of the person [conducting the search] and the categorization and classification system used to identify books and articles."

A few academic respondents expressed dissatisfaction with their lack of control over their own institutions and their individual careers. One of the milder comments compared universities to family-run law firms "where departments are groups of senior partners who have the discretion to conduct their academic lives as they see fit, while junior faculty put in long hours with little sense that their efforts will be evaluated fairly."

Many respondents took this opportunity to talk about the things that are keeping them from fulfilling their goals as scholars: the inadequacy of faculty salaries, the heavy teaching loads that keep them from doing research, and the funding and publication problems faced by scholars who are not using currently popular research methodologies or whose research area is not currently in vogue.

While 82 percent of respondents working outside of an academic institution report they have access to a library for the scholarly materials they need, some of the comments suggest that gaining access is not easy. One historian wrote: "In many places the unaffiliated scholar must jump through hoops for weeks and do battle fiercely to be allowed limited access to research materials. You literally have to call upon the 'big boys' to write on your behalf. And even then, the host institution sends you from office to office before they'll even issue you a library card. By the time you've succeeded or failed you feel like a tramp that's been turned away from a posh dinner party."

Software needs

Respondents noted that most computer programs are written for the hard sciences or for business and are difficult to adapt for the social sciences or humanities. Few are able to write programs themselves or can afford to take the time to learn this skill, consequently, the need for software written specifically for scholarly endeavors continues to grow. However, the software needs expressed in the survey reflect both the lack of software and the lack of information on what software is available. Some of the items listed do exist, but scholars have few sources for information on such programs. The software listed fell into three categories: teaching (26 percent), English and foreign language wordprocessing (37 percent), and research (37 percent).

Teaching software requests were for instructional software (especially interactive programs) specific to the scholarly disciplines. Political scientists and sociologists want software to help them teach data analysis and show students what happens when population parameters change. Historians would like programs that simulate historical periods, especially programs that allow students to change the parameters so they can see how historical outcomes might have been different given different conditions. Philosophers would like programs for teaching logic and ethics. Other respondents say they would like programs for teaching writing and bibliographic skills, drama, analyzing poetry, and teaching foreign languages.

Respondents express a need for word processing programs that are designed for scholars and have the ability to generate statistical tables and integrate them into the text. They also say they need bibliographic programs that allow more room for annotations, programs that renumber pages automatically, and indexing programs that will operate on personal computers.

In research, many respondents expressed the need for data management programs that allow analysis of textual materials and full text retrieval and that can operate on a microcomputer. Many also need data analysis programs that will run on computers that are not IBM or IBM-compatible.

Concluding Remarks

The ACLS survey provides a reading on the experience and attitudes of a cross-section of scholars in the mid-1980s. The findings draw together data on a wide range of issues that have been topics of research and of discussion in recent years and provide a benchmark in comparison with studies in the future.

These issues are related to what has become known in recent years as "the system of scholarly communication". As Robert M. Lumiansky, president of ACLS, wrote in 1979 in the Foreword to *Scholarly Communication: The Report of the National Enquiry:* "During the period of the Enquiry we came to realize more clearly than any of us had earlier realized the truth of one axiom: the various constituencies involved in scholarly communication—the scholars themselves, the publishers of books and of learned journals, the research librarians, the learned societies—are all components of a single system and are thus fundamentally dependent upon each other."

In recent years, this sense of interdependence, the recognition that what one constituency does affects the others, has led to efforts by people in all of these groups to acquaint others with their respective roles and problems. This survey was part of the program of the American Council of Learned Societies to contribute to that process of mutual understanding.

Appendixes

A. Appendix Tables, A-1 to A-30
B. Technical Appendix
C. Survey Questionnaire

Table A-1. Response rate for sampled societies

Discipline	Society	Membership	Number mailed	Valid returns	Response rate
Literature	Modern Language Association*	9,100	915	636	69.5%
Classics	American Philological Association	1,950	633	451	71.2
Philosophy	American Philosophical Association	5,500	658	481	73.3
History	American Historical Association	10,850	855	611	71.6
	Organization of American Historians	5,612			
Linguistics	Linguistic Society of America	2,100	667	493	73.9
Political Science	American Political Science Association	5,500	833	575	69.0
Sociology	American Sociological Association	9,000	824	588	71.4
	Totals		5,385	3,835	71.2

*Only those members of the Modern Language Association who teach English or American Literature were included in the sample. These scholars total 9,100 of the MLA's 25,000 members.

Table A-2. on facing page ──────────────────────────▶

Table A-3. Profile of society members in sample
(Percentages)

Employment	All	Academic[a]	Nonacademic[a]
Full time	91	94	80
Half-time or more	5	4	8
Less than half-time	5	2	12
Highest degree			
Doctorate	86	92	62
Professional	1	1	3
Masters	11	7	27
Bachelors or other	2	1	8
Society memberships			
One	8	7	12
2-3	39	38	43
4-5	32	33	28
More than 5	21	22	17
Society activities during past 3 years			
Attended meeting	88	93	75
Gave paper	63	70	41
On panel	51	56	34
Chaired committee	34	37	22
Served as officer	21	23	14

Maximum N = 3835
Percentages may not add to 100 because of rounding
[a]Excluding retirees

Table A-2. *Weighting of sample: Size of society memberships and number of respondents*

Society	Number of domestic members	Percentage of combined memberships	Number of respondents	Percentage of sample	Weight factors	Number of weighted respondents	Percentage of weighted sample
MLA, Literature*	9,100	20.7%	636	16.6%	1.247	792	20.7%
Philology	1,950	4.4	451	11.7	.376	169	4.4
Philosophy	5,500	12.5	481	12.6	.992	480	12.5
History**	10,850	24.7	611	15.9	1.553	945	24.7
Linguistics	2,100	4.8	493	12.8	.375	184	4.8
Political Science	5,500	12.5	575	15.0	.833	480	12.5
Sociology	9,000	20.5	588	15.3	1.339	788	20.5
Totals	44,000	100	3,835	100		3,838	100

*Only those members of the Modern Language Association who teach English or American Literature were included in the sample.

**The size of the American Historical Association membership was used in weighting, though members of Organization of American Historians are also included in the sample.

Number of weighted respondents is not identical with number of respondents because of rounding. Percentages may not add to 100 because of rounding.

Table A-4. Profile of respondents employed at universities and colleges, by discipline

Category	All	Literature	Classics	Philosophy	History	Linguistics	Political Science	Sociology
Type of academic institution[a]								
Total	100%	100%	100%	100%	100%	100%	100%	100%
Research university	39	36	47	32	33	64	42	46
Ph.D. granting university	14	13	17	12	16	14	13	13
Comprehensive institution	23	25	15	28	24	12	26	20
Liberal arts college	17	17	17	21	20	8	16	14
Two-year institution	4	5	1	5	5	1	1	5
Other	2	4	2	2	2	1	2	2
Public	60	61	46	55	59	69	61	67
Private	40	39	54	45	41	31	39	33
Institution's selectivity in admitting undergraduates[b]								
Most selective	23	20	36	20	20	29	28	22
Moderately selective	45	46	39	46	44	42	41	50
Not very selective	30	32	22	33	32	24	29	26
Highest degree								
Ph.D.	92	91	94	93	90	96	94	89
Other	8	9	6	7	10	4	6	11
Faculty rank								
Full professor	41	39	36	42	48	38	43	37
Associate professor	30	29	31	29	28	30	30	35
Assistant professor	23	24	27	21	18	26	23	22
Lecturer, instructor, etc.	6	7	6	7	6	6	4	6
Tenure status								
Tenured	66	66	65	69	71	64	67	64
Nontenured, on tenure track	18	18	19	16	13	19	19	20
Nontenured, nontenure track	12	11	13	13	13	14	10	12
Other	4	5	3	3	5	3	4	4

Percentages may not add to 100 because of rounding

[a]The classifications used in this survey are based on definitions published by the Carnegie Council on Policy Studies in Higher Education. Elsewhere in this report, two categories—institutions granting the doctorate and comprehensive colleges and universities—are combined.

[b]Selectivity judged by respondent. Top groupings combine two choices in question:
Most selective = "extremely" and "very selective"
Moderately selective = "selective" and "somewhat selective"

Category	All	Literature	Classics	Philosophy	History	Linguistics	Political Science	Sociology
Type of student taught								
At least half graduate students	25	17	24	19	18	57	34	38
Mostly undergraduates	37	43	40	29	46	31	36	29
All undergraduates	37	40	36	51	35	12	29	34
Mean yearly course load								
(Courses, semester basis)	5.4	5.8	5.4	5.8	5.6	4.9	5.3	5.0
Personal disciplinary approach								
Same as that of the society[c]	n.a.	81	79	94	92	86	91	86
Other	n.a.	19	21	6	8	14	9	14
Humanities	45	86	80	68	50	19	8	3
Social sciences	24	1	1	2	10	33	59	63
Use each equally	17	4	11	9	29	24	22	19
Reject distinction	13	8	6	20	11	23	10	14
Mean age (years)	45.6	46.0	45.4	45.4	47.8	45.0	44.9	44.9
Sex								
Male	75	62	73	82	81	64	87	74
Female	25	38	27	18	19	36	13	26
Race								
White	95	97	98	97	97	90	92	92
Other	5	3	2	3	3	10	8	8
Total family income								
Up to $34,000	30	33	33	35	25	31	24	28
$35,000 to $49,000	28	27	31	30	23	28	29	25
$50,000 to $64,000	22	21	20	19	25	24	20	23
$65,000 +	22	19	16	17	26	18	27	23
Consultancies in past three years								
None	58	64	74	66	59	50	52	41
Yes, average of $1000 or less annually	29	28	20	27	29	39	26	34
Yes, more than $1000 a year	13	8	6	7	12	12	22	25
Size of maximum sample	*3002*	*536*	*340*	*423*	*406*	*403*	*469*	*425*

[c]Thus a scholar who was included in the sample from the American Political Science Association chooses political science as the discipline that best represents his or her scholarly discipline.

Table A-5.   Comparison of female and male respondents, by discipline and stage of career

(Percentages)

Type of respondent	Female	Male
All respondents	26	74
Nonacademic	33	67
Academic	25	75
All respondents, by discipline		
Literature	38	62
Classics	27	73
Philosophy	17	83
History	21	79
Linguistics	36	64
Political Science	15	85
Sociology	30	70
Academic respondents by stage of career		
Began before 1965	8	92
Began 1965-69	15	85
Began 1970-74	24	76
Began 1975-79	31	69
Began 1980-85	36	64

N = 3799

Table A-6.   Changes in journal subscriptions

Question: Are you subscribing to the same number of journals subscribed to during the preceding year, or have you increased or decreased the number of your subscriptions?

(Percentages)

Type of respondent	Response			
	Same	Increased	Decreased	Not sure
All respondents	67	19	13	1
Nonacademic	67	19	14	*
Academic	67	20	13	*
Stage of career:				
Began before 1965	78	10	11	*
Began in 1980-85	58	30	11	1
Research University	67	21	12	*
College	69	17	13	1
Female	64	23	12	1
Male	67	19	13	1

N = 3813

*Less than one percent

Percentages may not add to 100 because of rounding

Table A-7.   **Readership of selected general periodicals, by discipline and type of institution**
Question: *During the past year, have you read any of the following literary or scientific publications [regularly or occasionally] aimed at a broad audience?*

(Percentages)

Type of respondents	Book review publications[a] Reg.	Occ.	Chronicle of Higher Educ. Reg.	Occ.	Science publications[b] Reg.	Occ.	American Scholar Reg.	Occ.
All respondents	50	32	24	38	16	27	5	16
Literature	62	29	27	44	10	21	6	22
Classics	44	36	17	37	9	22	6	16
Philosophy	49	35	19	41	24	33	2	15
History	56	31	31	34	11	19	7	19
Linguistics	32	36	15	32	27	33	2	7
Political Science	48	35	21	41	12	30	4	14
Sociology	38	32	22	35	22	36	3	10
Academic respondents	51	32	27	42	14	27	5	16
Research university	55	30	24	37	16	29	5	12
Ph.D. and comprehensive	49	33	27	45	14	23	4	18
College	49	36	32	46	10	28	5	20
Nonacademic	45	32	16	23	21	30	4	14
N =	3746		3626		3539		3408	

[a]*New York Times Book Review, Times Literary Supplement, New York Review of Books*

[b]*Science, Scientific American, Technology Today, Science 85*

Note: Respondents were also asked whether they read *Humanities,* published by the National Endowment for the Humanities; 3 percent said "yes, regularly" and 10 percent "yes, occasionally."

Table A-8.   Keeping up with the literature, by discipline, type of institution, and stage of career

Question: It is virtually impossible to even minimally keep up with the literature in my field.

(Percentages)

Type of respondents	Agree[b]	Disagree[c]	Neutral or not sure	Total
All respondents[a]	58	26	15	100
Literature	63	21	15	100
Classics	52	31	16	100
Philosophy	59	26	15	100
History	57	28	15	100
Linguistics	61	22	16	100
Political Science	58	29	13	100
Sociology	57	27	16	100
Academic	58	28	14	100
Research universities	53	32	14	100
Ph.D. granting and comprehensive	60	25	14	100
Colleges	64	24	12	100
Stage of career				
Began before 1965	64	24	12	100
Began 1965-69	56	29	16	100
Began 1970-74	58	27	13	100
Began 1975-79	56	30	13	100
Began 1980-85	54	30	17	100

N = 3792

Percentages may not add to 100 because of rounding
[a]About one percent checked "no opinion"
[b]About one in three said they "strongly agree"
[c]About one in seven said they "strongly disagree"

Table A-9. **Opinions on value of articles in major journal, by discipline and stage of career**

Question: *When I look at a new issue of my discipline's major journal, I rarely find an article that interests me.*

(Percentages)

Type of respondents	Agree[a]	Disagree[b]	Neutral or not sure
All respondents	33	55	12
Literature	37	53	10
Classicists	23	63	14
Philosophy	23	67	9
History	29	58	13
Linguistics	19	66	15
Political Science	43	45	12
Sociology	41	44	13
Nonacademic	37	51	12
Academic	33	55	12
Stage of career:			
Began before 1965	32	57	11
Began 1965-69	32	56	11
Began 1970-74	39	49	12
Began 1975-79	35	53	12
Began 1980-85	31	56	12

N = 3794
Percentages may not add to 100 because of rounding
[a]Includes those who "strongly agree"
[b]Includes those who "strongly disagree"

Table A-10. *Estimated number of articles published during career in a referred journal, by discipline and stage of career*

(Percentage of respondents publishing each quantity)

Type of respondent	None	One	2–4	5–9	10–19	20 or more	Mean number published
All respondents	27	19	19	15	13	7	5.3
Discipline							
Literature	27	19	19	15	14	7	5.4
Classics	26	21	17	15	12	9	5.9
Philosophy	24	19	15	18	14	9	6.1
History	34	20	19	12	10	5	4.1
Linguistics	20	18	23	17	13	9	6.2
Political Science	27	18	20	16	13	5	4.7
Sociology	22	19	19	14	15	10	6.3
Nonacademic	47	18	18	9	6	2	2.6
Academic	23	19	19	16	15	8	6.0
Stage of career:							
Began before 1965	12	20	14	13	23	18	9.6
Began 1965-69	14	16	15	19	21	14	8.8
Began 1970-74	14	19	21	19	17	9	6.6
Began 1975-79	18	15	22	24	15	5	5.5
Began 1980-85	31	24	25	13	6	1	2.7

N = *3604*   Percentages may not add to 100 because of rounding.

Table A-11. *Percentage of respondents who have written for general publications, by discipline and stage of career*

Type of respondent	Essay or article in newspaper, magazine	Book review in newspaper, magazine	Novel, short stories or poetry
All respondents	39	27	13
Literature	41	39	30
Classics	27	16	13
Philosophy	33	22	9
History	45	35	7
Linguistics	24	11	13
Political Science	51	26	6
Sociology	30	16	8
Nonacademic	39	21	11
Academic	38	28	13
Stage of career:			
Began before 1965	50	50	14
Began 1965-69	44	32	18
Began 1970-74	39	27	10
Began 1975-79	33	20	9
Began 1980-85	30	19	13

Maximum N = *3430*

Table A-12. **Publication of dissertation, by discipline and stage of career**

Question: *Have you published all or part of your dissertation in the original or in a revised form (excluding microform copy in University Microfilm)?*

Type of respondent	Published all or most as book	Published part as book or article	Published none of it	Did not write a dissertation
All respondents	22	33	36	9
Literature	22	33	37	8
Classics	27	29	37	7
Philosophy	11	34	51	4
History	35	26	26	14
Linguistics	24	36	34	6
Political Science	19	36	37	8
Sociology	13	39	37	11
Nonacademic	12	22	38	28
Academic	23	36	36	5
Stage of career:				
Began before 1965	34	34	32	*
Began 1965-69	30	38	32	*
Began 1970-74	24	41	35	*
Began 1975-79	28	38	34	*
Began 1980-85	13	38	48	*

*Less than one percent
N = 3699
Percentages may not add to 100 because of rounding.

Table A-13. **Prevalence of bias in peer review**

Question: *How often, if at all, do you think the peer review refereeing system for scholarly journals in your field is biased in favor of the following categories of people?*

(Percentage of all respondents)

Group favored	Rarely or never	Infrequently	Occasionally	Frequently	Not sure
Established researchers in a scholarly specialty	4	5	22	50	19
Scholars from prestigious institutions	6	8	24	41	22
Males	23	13	11	13	39
Scholars who use "currently fashionable approaches"	3	5	22	50	20

Maximum N = 3655
Percentages may not add to 100 because of rounding.

Table A-14. *Perceived frequency of bias in favor of established researchers in a scholarly specialty, by discipline and sex[1]*

(Percentage of all respondents)

Type of respondent	Rarely or never	Infrequently	Occasionally	Frequently	Not sure
All respondents	4	5	22	50	19
Literature	3	5	21	52	19
Classics	6	4	21	45	23
Philosophy	4	5	19	54	18
History	4	5	22	43	25
Linguistics	4	5	22	48	20
Political Science	5	4	24	51	16
Sociology	4	5	23	56	12
Nonacademic	1	4	17	50	28
Academic	4	5	23	51	16
Female	1	3	17	63	16
Male	5	5	26	47	17

$N = 3655$

Percentages may not add to 100 because of rounding.

[1]The responses are virtually identical to the related question about bias in favor of scholars using "currently fashionable" approaches.

Table A-15. *Perceived frequency of bias in favor of scholars from prestigious institutions, by discipline and sex*

(Percentages)

Type of respondent	Rarely or never	Infrequently	Occasionally	Frequently	Not sure
All respondents	6	8	24	41	22
Literature	4	8	24	41	23
Classics	8	9	24	33	26
Philosophy	4	7	23	44	22
History	5	8	22	38	27
Linguistics	8	10	24	32	27
Political Science	8	8	22	42	19
Sociology	6	7	27	46	14
Nonacademic	3	6	21	41	30
Academic	6	8	24	42	20
Female	3	6	20	51	21
Male	7	9	26	38	19

$N = 3641$

Percentages may not add to 100 because of rounding.

Table A-16. *Perceived frequency of bias in favor of males, by discipline and sex*

Type of respondent	Rarely or never	Infrequently	Occasionally	Frequently	Not sure
All respondents	23	13	11	13	39
Literature	20	13	13	16	38
Classics	29	13	9	10	39
Philosophy	24	10	11	13	42
History	20	12	11	13	45
Linguistics	27	13	8	9	44
Political Science	32	13	9	9	38
Sociology	22	16	14	16	31
Nonacademic	17	11	12	14	47
Academic	25	14	11	13	37
Female	8	11	17	32	32
Male	30	15	10	7	38

$N = 3588$
Percentages may not add to 100 because of rounding.

Table A-17.   Use of computerized catalogues at academic institutions
(Percentages)

Questions	All	Research universities	Ph.D.-granting/ comprehensive	Colleges
Has all or part of your library's card catalogue been computerized?				
Yes	40	59	33	17
Probably yes	6	6	5	4
Probably not	5	4	6	6
No	41	23	47	67
Do not know	8	9	9	6
Total	100	100	100	100
(About one-half (1430) of the academic respondents answered the following question)				
If yes, have you used the computerized catalogue?				
Yes	60	62	60	43
No	40	38	40	57

(Since only one-third of the academic respondents answered the following five questions, only the results for all academics are reported)

	Significantly	Moderately	A little	Not at all	Do not know
If yes, has this:					
Decreased your use of the card catalogue?	24%	17%	19%	37%	3%
Increased your access to scholarly materials?	12	20	20	41	6
Increased your productivity as a teacher?	4	11	15	63	7
Increased your research productivity?	6	14	19	54	6
Made the use of the library more enjoyable?	13	19	21	43	4

Maximum N = 2866

Percentages may not add to 100 because of rounding.

Table A-18 **Use of computerized database searches at academic institutions**

(Percentages)

Questions	All academics	Research universities	Ph.D.-granting/ comprehensive	Colleges
Total	100	100	100	100
How familiar are you with computerized database searches?				
Know little about them	34	35	31	36
Familiar but have not used	25	26	26	23
Have used once or twice	24	22	26	22
Have used several times	13	13	12	14
Have used frequently	5	5	4	4
Are searches available to you at your institution?				
Yes	62	67	64	55
Probably yes	18	19	17	15
Probably not	3	2	3	4
No	4	1	3	11
Have no idea	13	12	14	14
(One third [1055] of academic respondents answered the following questions)				
Who does your searching?				
Librarian, but I am present	42	38	44	46
Librarian, without my being present	36	32	39	39
Sometimes I do, sometimes a librarian	14	21	11	9
I always do it	6	7	4	5
Other	2	2	2	1
Who pays for your searches? (Respondents were asked for the answer that best represented their experience)				
I paid out of my pocket	21	22	23	11
They were charged to my grant	9	17	5	5
My department paid for them	20	22	20	19
Library or institution paid	39	28	41	56
Part out of pocket; part other	9	9	9	8
Other	2	2	2	2
How satisfied were you with the results of your most recent searches?				
Very satisfied	22	19	21	29
Mildly satisfied	49	49	49	48
Neutral	11	12	9	11
Mildly unsatisfied	13	15	15	7
Very unsatisfied	5	4	6	6
Not sure	0	0	1	0

Maximum N = 2933

Percentages may not add to 100 because of rounding.

Table A-19.   *Training in using library services at academic institutions*
(Percentages)

Questions	All academics	Research universities	Ph.D.-granting/ comprehensive	Colleges
Total	100	100	100	100
Does your college or university provide an opportunity for you to learn about the new technical services available in the library?				
Yes	54	67	49	43
No	46	33	51	57
Is there a library orientation or instruction program for:				
Freshmen				
Yes	78	74	80	87
No	3	2	3	4
Not sure	18	24	17	9
Junior-senior students				
Yes	37	42	33	36
No	19	9	23	36
Not sure	44	49	44	28
Graduate students				
Yes	40	51	31	23
No	17	8	21	44
Not sure	43	41	48	33

Maximum N = 2819

Percentages may not add to 100 because of rounding.

Table A-20. **Quality of library services at academic institutions**
(Percentages)

Criteria	All academics	Research universities	Ph.D.-granting/ comprehensive	Colleges
Total	100	100	100	100
Ability to meet my needs through interlibrary loans				
Very good or excellent	66	68	65	67
Good	18	15	19	21
Fair or poor	10	9	12	9
Not sure	5	7	4	3
Quality and availability of microform reading machines				
Very good or excellent	47	54	43	45
Good	23	18	26	26
Fair or poor	19	14	22	21
Not sure	11	15	9	8
Access to computerized bibliographic databases				
Very good or excellent	43	50	38	42
Good	20	18	23	18
Fair or poor	20	14	22	24
Not sure	17	17	17	15
Ability to meet my research needs through book holdings				
Very good or excellent	32	51	20	19
Good	22	22	24	24
Fair or poor	45	26	55	57
Not sure	1	1	—	—
Ability to meet my research needs through journal holdings				
Very good or excellent	41	62	28	25
Good	23	19	28	24
Fair or poor	35	17	44	51
Not sure	1	1	—	—

Maximum N = 2930

Percentages may not add to 100 because of rounding.

Table A-21. *Convenience of library services at academic institutions*
(Percentages)

Questions	All academics	Research universities	Ph.D.-granting/ comprehensive	Colleges
Total	100	100	100	100

Respondents were asked how often they were inconvenienced by:

Waiting in long lines for books or equipment

Very often	1	2	1	0
Often	3	4	3	1
Moderately often	9	13	7	4
Seldom	30	34	32	17
Very seldom	56	45	56	78

Malfunctioning equipment

Very often	1	2	1	0
Often	4	5	5	2
Moderately often	14	15	15	11
Seldom	33	33	36	26
Very seldom	40	37	38	55

Inadequate facilities for reading journals

Very often	3	4	3	2
Often	5	5	6	3
Moderately often	13	13	14	11
Seldom	26	28	29	15
Very seldom	50	47	46	65

Inability to get help from librarians

Very often	1	1	1	1
Often	3	4	3	3
Moderately often	10	11	10	7
Seldom	28	28	31	21
Very seldom	56	53	53	67

Maximum N = 2916

Percentages may not add to 100 because of rounding.

Table A-22. **Importance of sources of materials at academic institutions**

(Percentages)

Questions	All institutions	Research universities	Ph.D.-granting/ comprehensive	Colleges
Total	100	100	100	100

How important are the following sources for keeping up in your field, teaching or research

Materials in personal library

	All institutions	Research universities	Ph.D.-granting/ comprehensive	Colleges
Great importance	76	80	75	72
Moderate importance	20	17	21	24
Slight importance	3	2	4	4
Little importance or did not use	—	—	—	—

Materials purchased during the past year

Great importance	62	65	62	60
Moderate importance	27	26	28	26
Slight importance	9	8	9	11
Little importance or did not use	2	1	2	2

Colleagues' copies

Great importance	6	8	5	4
Moderate importance	20	24	18	18
Slight importance	41	41	39	41
Little importance or did not use	33	26	39	36

Materials in institution's library

Great importance	48	59	43	39
Moderate importance	36	31	39	42
Slight importance	13	9	15	16
Little importance or did not use	3	2	3	3

Materials obtained through inter-library loan

Great importance	27	23	31	32
Moderate importance	24	24	24	27
Slight importance	22	24	21	19
Little importance or did not use	27	29	24	22

Materials identified through a computerized data base search

Great importance	7	6	6	9
Moderate importance	12	12	12	15
Slight importance	20	22	18	21
Little importance or did not use	61	60	64	55

Maximum N = 2969

Percentages may not add to 100 because of rounding.

Table A-23.   *Microfiche use at academic institutions*

(Percentages)

Question	All institutions	Research universities	Ph.D.-granting/ comprehensive	Colleges
Total	100	100	100	100
How familiar are you with microfiche?				
Know little about them	12	12	12	10
Familiar with them but have not used microfiche	10	10	10	12
Have used them once or twice	26	25	25	26
Have used them several times	34	31	36	35
Have used them frequently	19	22	17	17

Maximum N = 2944

Percentages may not add to 100 because of rounding.

Table A-24. **Computer familiarity, and hardware and software used**

(Percentage of respondents by discipline, employment, sex, and stage of career)

Category	ALL RESPONDENTS										ACADEMIC RESPONDENTS		Began teaching				
	All	Literature	Classics	Philosophy	History	Linguistics	Political Science	Sociology	Academic	Non-academic	Female	Male	Before 1965	1965–1969	1970–1974	1975–1979	1980–1985
Percentage of computing done personally																	
All	42	51	58	52	43	46	36	31	42	46	45	41	30	35	43	42	49
Some or most	42	33	28	35	38	45	47	52	42	40	41	42	39	45	42	49	43
Little or none	15	16	14	11	19	9	17	16	15	14	12	16	29	21	14	10	8
Make of PC used																	
Apple IIe	10	10	7	7	11	6	12	12	10	12	6	12	8	9	16	11	7
Macintosh	9	8	22	11	7	12	7	7	9	7	10	8	9	6	7	11	9
Osborn/Kaypro	14	18	12	17	12	12	11	11	14	11	17	13	11	12	13	15	17
IBM PC	22	24	23	21	23	18	20	22	22	20	21	23	32	26	22	16	22
IBM AT or XT	6	2	6	4	7	7	10	9	6	8	6	6	6	6	5	8	6
IBM compatible	12	11	8	12	10	13	12	14	12	11	12	12	7	12	10	16	15
Other	27	26	21	28	29	31	28	25	26	30	28	26	28	27	28	24	24
Types of programs owned[a]																	
Database	41	30	35	39	38	44	43	53	39	52	35	40	32	44	37	38	40
Combined database and wordprocessing	20	20	26	14	19	19	19	26	21	18	21	21	20	22	20	23	18
Spreadsheet	38	29	22	38	32	31	44	54	36	47	33	38	32	37	38	40	33
Combined wordprocessing, other functions	21	13	14	17	22	22	26	29	19	31	19	19	12	18	17	21	22
Wordprocessing	86	88	79	90	83	83	85	85	86	85	84	87	83	89	86	85	89
Statistical analysis	21	8	7	7	12	14	33	48	20	27	17	21	20	14	20	20	20
Have a modem:																	
Yes	29	17	20	27	18	38	36	48	29	32	26	31	19	32	28	33	32
No	71	83	80	73	82	62	64	52	71	68	64	69	81	68	72	67	68

Percentages may not add to 100 because of rounding.　　[a] On average, respondents own two programs or more.　　*Maximum N = 2654*

Table A-25. Comparison of computer uses

(Percentage of respondents by discipline, employment, sex, and stage of career)

Uses	All	Literature	Classics	Philosophy	History	Linguistics	Political Science	Sociology	Academic	Nonacademic	Female	Male	Before 1965	1965–1969	1970–1974	1975–1979	1980–1985
	ALL RESPONDENTS										**ACADEMIC RESPONDENTS**		Began teaching				
General wordprocessing	94	97	94	95	97	96	94	91	95	95	96	94	94	93	95	97	95
Maintaining curriculum vitae	71	75	69	76	64	79	71	71	73	61	77	73	64	70	77	77	79
Maintaining note files	54	58	57	63	49	69	48	50	53	58	59	51	46	46	50	58	58
Compiling a bibliography or index	49	54	47	46	50	56	47	46	48	52	54	46	50	42	52	46	48
Test preparation	49	56	55	61	37	60	49	44	53	27	55	53	41	52	51	57	58
Statistical analysis	42	12	13	8	30	41	62	82	39	56	41	39	34	34	40	43	40
Preparing charts, diagrams or graphics	25	16	13	11	16	30	31	43	21	44	24	21	19	15	24	22	21
Preparing budgets	21	16	15	18	20	19	24	28	18	38	18	18	18	19	20	18	14
Accessing online databases through service networks	20	19	13	15	17	14	25	25	18	26	22	17	21	17	17	15	18
Using library's online catalogue	17	22	20	12	16	17	16	17	17	15	18	18	20	20	20	18	15
Computer-assisted teaching	17	14	19	16	10	16	20	24	18	10	18	19	14	15	20	22	17
Preparing concordances, dictionaries, critical editions, etc.	14	20	25	10	16	29	9	8	13	21	14	12	15	11	14	11	9
Grading tests or papers	13	12	8	11	8	15	14	18	13	7	14	14	10	16	14	14	14
Electronic mail within my institution	11	9	8	6	8	24	11	15	10	14	10	11	6	8	12	12	11
Electronic mail with those outside my institution	9	3	7	6	5	23	11	13	8	15	6	8	5	6	6	8	10
Theme, text, semantic or language analysis	7	10	20	4	4	32	5	5	7	10	9	7	9	9	6	6	7

Maximum N = 2407

Table A-26.   *Computer access and experience*

(Percentage of respondents by employment, sex, stage of career, and type of institution)

Access and use	ALL RESPONDENTS				ACADEMIC RESPONDENTS							
					Began teaching							
	Academic	Non-academic	Female	Male	Pre-1965	1965–1969	1970–1974	1975–1979	1980–1985	Research university	Ph.D. granting/ comprehensive institution	Liberal Arts College
Access to a computer												
Yes	96%	86%	97%	96%	96%	96%	96%	97%	97%	98%	96%	96%
No	4	14	3	4	4	4	4	3	3	2	4	4
Routinely use a computer*	53	48	56	53	42	50	57	53	65	57	51	51
Occasionally use	19	20	17	19	16	20	21	25	16	23	18	15
Do not use	28	32	27	28	42	30	22	22	19	20	31	34
Have computer for exclusive use:	48	41	53	47	38	52	53	54	52	56	44	45
At home	32	25	38	30	26	33	36	34	32	34	30	30
At office	8	6	8	8	7	8	7	9	12	10	7	10
Both places	8	11	7	9	5	10	11	11	9	12	7	6
Fair to excellent skill in:												
Touch typing	86	87	92	84	82	87	88	88	87	86	85	87
Word processing	62	64	67	61	42	58	68	70	76	69	58	58
Computer programming	20	32	19	21	10	15	22	26	28	24	17	17
Place of nearest computer												
In own office	30	54	30	30	25	29	27	36	33	38	25	25
In nearby office	40	27	35	41	41	41	42	38	39	39	45	35
Elsewhere	31	20	35	29	35	30	30	25	28	24	30	40
Used computers in graduate school	24	34	27	24	3	14	18	30	47	30	23	17
Have written a computer program												
for research	12	24	11	13	6	9	13	16	15	16	11	7
for teaching	9	9	5	10	5	8	11	9	10	9	10	9

*including use by assistant   *Maximum N* = 3782

Table A-27.   Anticipated effect of computers on the intellectual progress of the discipline over the next five years
(Percentage of respondents by discipline, employment, sex, and stage of career)

Choices	ALL RESPONDENTS										ACADEMIC RESPONDENTS						
	All	Literature	Classics	History	Philosophy	Linguistics	Political Science	Sociology	Academic	Nonacademic	Female	Male	Began teaching				
													Before 1965	1965–1969	1970–1974	1975–1979	1980–1985
Very positive	18%	17%	16%	9%	15%	31%	17%	27%	18%	23%	20%	17%	12%	16%	18%	15%	24%
Positive	46	43	45	42	48	46	49	45	46	48	44	47	46	49	48	44	45
Neutral	23	27	23	34	23	16	20	16	25	16	23	25	26	27	23	28	21
Negative*	5	4	6	4	5	1	8	7	5	5	5	5	6	2	5	5	5
Don't know	9	10	11	11	10	6	6	6	8	8	8	6	10	5	7	8	4

*Includes "very negative"   N = 3709

Table A-28. Anticipated effect of computers on how the discipline is taught over the next five years
(Percentage of respondents by discipline, employment, sex, and stage of career)

Choices	ALL RESPONDENTS												ACADEMIC RESPONDENTS				
													Began teaching				
	All	Literature	Classics	Philosophy	History	Linguistics	Political Science	Sociology	Academic	Nonacademic	Female	Male	Before 1965	1965-1969	1970-1974	1975-1979	1980-1985
Very positive	8%	8%	6%	3%	5%	10%	7%	13%	7%	12%	8%	7%	5%	5%	7%	7%	10%
Positive	34	31	27	26	28	37	40	43	34	32	32	35	33	36	38	31	35
Neutral	38	39	45	52	40	36	34	25	40	28	40	40	39	44	36	45	39
Negative*	7	6	6	6	9	2	8	7	6	8	5	8	8	6	7	6	6
Don't know	14	15	16	14	17	15	10	12	12	20	14	11	15	8	11	12	11

*Includes "very negative"   N = 3686

Table A-29.   *Professional reading of retired and employed respondents*

(Percentage who read and average number of publications read per respondent)

Type of publication	Retired	Academics	Nonacademics
Journal subscriptions			
none or one	14%	8%	12%
two or three	39	31	39
four or more	47	62	50
average number	3.8	4.8	4.2
Additional journals examined regularly			
none	45%	33%	37%
one or two	17	19	20
three or more	38	49	43
average number	2.9	3.7	3.8
Journals examined at least once a year			
none	17%	9%	19%
one or two	24	15	17
three or more	58	76	64
Scholarly books purchased			
none to four	31%	12%	24%
five to nine	23	15	20
ten to nineteen	25	28	27
twenty or more	21	45	30
average number	13.3	22.1	16.3

Percentages may not add to 100 because of rounding.

Maximum N of retirees = 158

Table A-30. Publications reported by retirees and other respondents

| | Retired | | Academics who began career before 1965 | | All academics | | Nonacademics | |
Type of publication	Percent who published	Average number	Percent who published	Average number	Percent who published	Average number	Percent who published	Average number
Textbook	39%	1.0	35%	.7	16%	.3	7%	.1
Scholarly book (editor)	100	3.2	49	1.1	28	.5	17	.3
Scholarly book (author)	100	3.2	72	1.9	45	.9	28	.4
Chapter in scholarly book	100	4.1	75	2.8	55	1.7	36	.9
Article in scholarly journal	100	12.3	88	9.6	77	6.0	53	2.6
Comment in scholarly journal	100	4.5	44	.9	28	.6	20	.3
Book review in scholarly journal	81	9.5	88	11.0	70	5.2	42	1.9
Paper in conference proceedings	68	3.6	74	3.7	61	2.8	48	1.8

Maximum N of retirees 158

Technical Appendix
By Robert Cameron Mitchell

The Sample

A stratified random sample design was used for this study. Seven disciplines represented in the American Council of Learned Societies were selected so that together they would be reasonably representative of scholars in the humanities and social sciences. The current membership (excluding graduate students and foreign members) of the appropriate society or, in the case of history, two societies, was used as a sampling frame, as shown in appendix table A-1. Samples were drawn by taking every *nth* name from the society's membership file so that a target sample size of at least 650 per discipline would be achieved. The target was chosen by balancing cost against the need to have a sufficient number of respondents for each society to be able to meaningfully generalize to that society's total membership. The sample sizes varied from 633 in classics to 915 in literature.

Three sets of identical mailing labels were used to elicit responses. The mailings began with a post card timed to arrive one week in advance of the survey which informed the selected society member of the forthcoming questionnaire and appealed for his or her cooperation. The second mailing was a package mailed first-class that contained a cover letter, a copy of the questionnaire, a return envelope with first class postage in stamps affixed to it, and a stamped postcard that the respondents were invited to fill out with their name and address and mail in when they returned the questionnaire. Respondents were offered the opportunity to receive a brief summary of the findings by checking the appropriate box on the postcard. This system allowed us to maintain anonymity while providing the opportunity to offer the study summary (which most respondents requested) and help to limit the followup mailings to the nonrespondents. The final mailing consisted of a followup reminder postcard mailed two weeks after the questionnaire to all those who had not returned a postcard. The first mailing was sent out in early November 1985. The last returns that were included in the data set were received before the end of January 1986.

The questionnaire (see appendix C) was typeset and printed as a stapled booklet of 16 pages. It contained a total of 229 ques-

tions (including part questions) arranged in five sections:
I. Personal and Institutional Background,   II. Library
Resources,   III. Professional Reading,   IV. Research and
Publication,   V. Computer Resources and Use,   VI. Sup-
plemental Information. The response rate varied somewhat by
society from 69 percent for the American Political Science
Association to 73.9 for the Linguistic Society of America (see
Appendix A, table A-1). For the entire sample the response rate,
after adjusting for a few in the sample found to be inappropriate
(because they were graduate students, deceased etc.) was 71.3
percent.

In generalizing from the responses given by a sample to the
population from which the sample was drawn—in this case, the
member societies—it is necessary to take various sources of error
into account. One potential source of error that should be borne
in mind in generalizing our findings is sample selection bias.
This bias, which is more likely to occur in mail surveys than in
telephone or in-person surveys, stems from the fact that people
can examine a mail questionnaire at their leisure before deciding
whether or not to respond. As a result, those who do choose to
respond may have a greater interest in the subject than those
who throw it in the wastebasket. In the case of this survey, for
example, those who do not own or use personal computers may
have been less likely to spend the time filling it out than those
who do use computers. If this is the case—and there is no way to
check this hypothesis short of conducting a special study—our
sample would overrepresent the computer users.

Even presuming that those who responded did *not* differ from
those who did on any variables of interest, random factors introduce sampling errors in surveys. The result is that the
responses of a randomly selected subset of a group's membership
will differ somewhat from the responses of the entire membership
if they were available. A major determinant of sampling error is
the absolute size of the usable responses or realized sample
(hereafter called the sample). For this survey the realized samples
ranged from 451 valid returns for the American Philological
Association to 636 for the Modern Language Association. A
crude but useful rule of thumb for taking this source of bias into
account is to regard each percentage reported in this study as the
midpoint of a range which will include the population percentage
95 times out of 100. How wide a range? The ability of a

400-person sample (presuming randomness in other respects) to accurately predict the responses for the population from which the sample was drawn is plus or minus 4–6 percentage points. In other words, if all 400 people answered a question about whether their library has a computerized card catalog and 41 percent said yes, the percent of the total population holding this view could be expected to lie between 35 and 47 percent (41 +/– 6 percent) ninety-five times out of one hundred. For a sample of 600 respondents, the margin of error would be 3–5 percent; at 1500 it becomes 2–3 percent.

When results are compared for two different groups of people in the sample—such as the American Sociological Association vs. the MLA or self-ascribed humanists vs. social scientists—the sampling error must be taken into account in determining whether a difference is statistically significant or not. If the two samples are each 600 in size, a difference of 7–8 percent[1] is required before the two groups' answers to a given question can be treated as significant. The finer the distinction that is made— young female sociologists vs. young female political scientists— the smaller the number of cases to be compared and the larger the percentage difference requires for significance. For example, a difference of ten to thirteen percentage points is needed in cases where each of the samples is 200 in size.

Together, the 3,835 respondents who returned the questionnaire represent the combined membership of eight scholarly societies. Since our sampling plan did not take the actual size of the societies into account—the 9,000 sociologist members of the American Sociological Association are represented in our sample by almost as many respondents, 588, as the 5,500 members of the American Political Science Association, 575—additional procedures are needed to avoid the possibility that our combined estimates may misrepresent in some manner the aggregate views of the almost 50,000 scholars who belong to the eight societies. As shown in appendix table A-2, linguists are overrepresented relative to their numbers while historians, sociologists, and MLA members are underrepresented. In order to make the sample more representative of the combined memberships, we weighted the data to compensate for the differential societal sampling rates. By this statistical procedure, each historian in the sample is made to stand for slightly more than one historian and each

---

1. Seven percent for percentages near 20 or 80; eight percent for percentages near 50.

linguist for slightly less than one linguist with the result that the weighted sample replicates the actual distribution of the societies' membership. As it turned out, the distortion is minimal. Careful comparison of the distribution of responses on each question for the weighted and unweighted samples shows extremely minor and never statistically significant differences between the two. For consistency, however, all findings in this report are based on the weighted sample except when the findings are presented by society when weighting is irrelevant.

The data from this study have been deposited in the Roper Center for use by scholars. Data tapes may be obtained by contacting the Center's librarian at:

The Roper Center
The University of Connecticut
341 Mansfield Rd.
U-164 Room 421
Storrs, CT 06268

SURVEY OF SCHOLARS
Office of Scholarly Communication and Technology
American Council of Learned Societies

November 8, 1985

To members of affiliated societies:

The American Council of Learned Societies is sponsoring a survey of scholars in cooperation with several of its affiliated societies, and you are one of 800 members of your society chosen at random to receive the enclosed questionnaire. We hope you will fill it out. Your participation is essential whether you are employed by an academic institution, government agency, or a nonprofit or business organization.

The survey covers questions about scholarly publication, access to library resources, and the uses and implications of new computer technology. Considerable change has occurred in each of these areas and rapid changes are anticipated in the future. The survey, which is one of the first of its kind, will enable us to take stock of these developments and how they are affecting scholars, such as yourself, and the scholarly community at large. We will send you a copy of the survey report if you indicate your interest on the enclosed postcard.

The confidentiality of your responses will be protected, and the results will be used for statistical purposes only. Our pretest indicates that filling out the questionnaire usually requires a half hour or less.

Please return the questionnaire in the enclosed envelope, which is stamped with first class postage. We hope you can find time to answer the questions and return the questionnaire within a week, if possible, after you receive it.

At the same time, fill out and return the reply card so that we will not trouble you with reminders. Note that there is a box to check if you want a copy of the survey report.

We will greatly appreciate receiving your response. If you have any questions, please call me at (202) 328-2431. Thank you.

Herbert C. Morton, *Director*
Office of Scholarly Communication

Participating societies:

American Historical Association
American Philological Association
American Philosophical Association
American Political Science Association

American Sociological Association
Linguistic Society of America
Modern Language Association of America
Organization of American Historians

SURVEY OF SCHOLARS
Office of Scholarly Communication and Technology
American Council of Learned Societies

Instructions: Please circle the number next to the most appropriate answer. This questionnaire is addressed to scholars who work in various settings; if certain questions do not pertain to your workplace, please skip them.

I. PERSONAL AND INSTITUTIONAL BACKGROUND

1. Which *one* of the following *best* describes your professional scholarly discipline? (circle one number)

   1 Classics   *5* Political Science
   2 English Literature   *6* Linguistics or languages
   3 History   *7* Sociology
   4 Philosophy   *8* Interdisciplinary or other (please specify): _____

2. Are you considered to be a full-time employee of your organization or school?

   1 Yes, full time
   2 No, part time, but more than half time
   3 No, half time
   4 No, less than half time
   5 No, graduate student

3. What is the highest academic degree you have completed?

   1 Bachelors (B.A., B.S., etc.)
   2 Masters (including work towards the Ph.D.)
   3 Professional degree (LL.B. etc.)
   4 Doctorate (Ph.D., Ed.D etc.)
   5 Other (please specify): _____

4. How many professional societies related to your scholarly discipline, research interest, or work do you currently belong to? Include all regional societies and specialist societies to which you currently pay dues.

       1 One   2 Two to three   3 Four to five   4 More than five

5. Considering only professional societies of the type described in question 4; over the past *three years* did you:

	Yes	No	Not sure
Attend a meeting of a professional society	*1*	*2*	*3*
Give a paper at a professional society meeting	*1*	*2*	*3*
Participate on a panel at a professional society meeting (including being a discussant or chairing a session, but not including giving a paper)	*1*	*2*	*3*
Chair or serve on a committee of a professional society	*1*	*2*	*3*
Serve as an officer of a professional society (including its sections)	*1*	*2*	*3*

6. People have differing views about their professional associations; please indicate your attitude toward each of the following statements.

	Strongly agree	Agree	Neutral	Disagree	Strongly disagree	Not sure
I get a good value for the money I spend to belong to my discipline's major professional association.	*1*	*2*	*3*	*4*	*5*	*6*
Attending this association's annual professional meetings is (would be) largely a waste of my time.	*1*	*2*	*3*	*4*	*5*	*6*

7. Which one of the following best describes your *primary* employment during the year beginning September 1985? (If you are on leave, provide the information for your permanent position.)

    1 Faculty member at a college or university

    2 Administrator at a college or university with faculty status

    3 Nonfaculty, affiliated with a college or university (e.g. administrative or research position without faculty status)

    4 Employed by private industry, or private or government library or research organization (e.g., consulting firm, nonprofit think tank etc.)

    5 Retired

    6 Other (please describe briefly): _____

◄ **Go to question 17 if not employed by a college or university.**

8. The Carnegie Commission on Higher Education has classified institutions of higher learning into the following categories. Which *one* best describes your college or university?

    1 **Research university** (Awards at least 50 Ph.D.'s a year.)

    2 **Ph.D. granting university** (Awards between 10 and 49 Ph.D.'s a year.)

    3 **Comprehensive college or university** (Offers a liberal arts program as well as one or more other degree programs, such as teacher training, engineering and business administration, which enroll a significant number of students. Awards very few, if any, Ph.D.'s.)

    4 **Liberal arts college** (Primarily grants liberal arts degrees although may grant a few masters or specialized degrees. If college is involved in teacher training, future teachers tend to receive their degrees in arts and sciences fields, rather than in education.

    5 **Two year colleges and institutes**

    6 **Other** (please describe or indicate name of institution): _____

9. Please characterize your institution on each of the following dimensions.

    Type: *1* Public   or   *2* Private

    Calendar: *1* On the semester (or 4-1-4) system
               2 On the quarter system
               3 On some other type of calendar

    Selectivity in admitting *undergraduate* students:
               1 Extremely selective
               2 Very selective
               3 Selective
               4 Somewhat selective
               5 Not very selective
               6 Uncertain how selective it is

10. What is your present rank?

    1 Instructor   *2* Lecturer   *3* Assistant professor   *4* Associate professor
          5 Full professor   *6* Other rank   *7* Do not hold rank designation

11. What is your tenure status?

    1 Tenured   *2* Nontenured in tenure track position   *3* Not on tenure track
          4 Other (please describe): _____

12. Please give the date (year) of the following:

Year received highest degree now held	Year joined present institution	Year obtained current rank	Year tenure first granted
19 __	19 __	19 __	19 __ (if not tenured, enter XX)

13. Does your department offer graduate degrees? (If you hold an appointment in more than one department answer for the one which offers the highest degree.)

    1 Yes, doctorate   *2* Yes, masters only   *3* No

14. Over the past three years what has been your mix of graduate (including dissertation and thesis supervision) and undergraduate teaching responsibilities?

    1 All graduate   *2* Mostly graduates   *3* Half of each   *4* Mostly undergraduate   *5* All undergraduate

15. What is your regular or normal *annual* teaching load?

_____ courses per year (counting each section of a large course you teach separately as a course)

16. Overall, how satisfied are you with your current job as a college teacher or administrator?

  1 Very satisfied   *2* Mildly satisfied   *3* Neutral   *4* Mildly unsatisfied   *5* Very unsatisfied   *6* Not sure

◄ **All Respondents**

17. How strong is the pressure at your institution for you to publish articles in scholarly journals and scholarly books?

  1 Extremely strong   *2* Strong   *3* Moderate   *4* Weak   *5* Very weak   *6* Not sure

18. Some scholars tend to think of themselves as humanists, others as social scientists. Which best describes how you approach your discipline?

  1 Mainly from the perspective of the humanities
  2 Mainly from the perspective of the social sciences
  3 Use each perspective about equally
  4 Don't regard the distinction as appropriate
  5 Not sure, don't know

II. LIBRARY RESOURCES

1. If you are *not* affiliated with an academic institution, do you currently have access to a library through which you can obtain some or all of the scholarly materials you need?

  1 Yes   *2* No   *3* Do not require scholarly materials

◄ **Go to question 15 if you do not have access to a library related to your work.**

2. Please give your personal rating of your institution's library (or library arrangements, if your institution gives you direct access to other libraries without going through interlibrary loan) on the following dimensions. If your institution has more than one library, give your rating of the overall library situation. Here as elsewhere, please skip questions which are not applicable to your situation.

	Excellent	Very good	Good	Fair	Poor	Not sure
Adequacy of *journal* holdings for MY specialized *research* needs	1	2	3	4	5	6
Adequacy of *journal* holdings for MY *teaching preparation* needs	1	2	3	4	5	6
Adequacy of *journal* holdings for STUDENT needs (including paper preparation)	1	2	3	4	5	6
Adequacy of *book* holdings for MY *research* needs	1	2	3	4	5	6
Adequacy of *book* holdings for MY *teaching* preparation needs	1	2	3	4	5	6
Adequacy of *book* holdings for my STUDENTS' needs (including paper preparation)	1	2	3	4	5	6
Adequacy of newspaper holdings	1	2	3	4	5	6
Adequacy of reference resources	1	2	3	4	5	6
Ability to meet my needs for articles and books by borrowing them through interlibrary loan	1	2	3	4	5	6
Quality and availability of machines needed to read microform (microfilm and microfiche) documents	1	2	3	4	5	6
Availability of trained reference librarians	1	2	3	4	5	6
Access to computerized bibliographic data bases	1	2	3	4	5	6

3. In using your institution's library, how often are you unnecessarily inconvenienced:

	Very often	Often	Moderately	Seldom	Very seldom	Do not use
By waiting in long lines for books or equipment	1	2	3	4	5	6
By malfunctioning equipment	1	2	3	4	5	6
By inadequate facilities for reading journals	1	2	3	4	5	6
By inability to get help from librarians	1	2	3	4	5	6

4. How familiar are you with *microfiche* (not microfilm)? (These are small card-size pieces of microfilm which are read by using a special microfiche reader.)

    1 Do not know very much about them
    2 Am familiar with them, but have never used them
    3 Have used them once or twice
    4 Have used them several times
    5 Have used them frequently

5. Does the library you use:

	Yes	Probably yes	Probably not	No	No idea
Have one or more microfiche readers which you can use?	1	2	3	4	5
Have materials in its collection (e.g. newspapers, magazines, books, dissertations) on microfiche which you have used or might want to use?	1	2	3	4	5

6. If you have used microfiche materials at least once in the last three years, indicate how satisfied you were the last time you used them with:

	Very satisfied	Mildly satisfied	Neutral	Mildly unsatisfied	Unsatisfied
The readability of the microfiche material?	1	2	3	4	5
The ease of access to a microfiche reader?	1	2	3	4	5
The ease of operation of the reader?	1	2	3	4	5
Your ability to obtain satisfactory paper copies from the microfiche?	1	2	3	4	5

7. How familiar are you with computerized searches of online data bases such as ERIC, MLA Bibliography, ABC/CLIO, Sociological Abstracts and so on, which are accessed by using a computer terminal to produce a customized list of references or sources on one or more topics chosen by the user.

    1 Do not know very much about them
    2 Am familiar with them, but have never used them
    3 Have used them once or twice
    4 Have used them several times
    5 Have used them frequently

8. Are such searches currently available to you at your institution (either free or for a fee) through your library, computer center, or your computer terminal.

    1 Yes   *2* Probably yes   *3* Probably not   *4* No   *5* No idea

◄ **If you have not used a bibliographic search at least once, skip to question 12.**

9. Does a librarian do the search for you or do you do the search directly on a computer terminal (whether in the library or not)?

    1 A librarian always does it, but I am usually present during the search
    2 A librarian always does it without my being present
    3 Sometimes I do it, sometimes a librarian does it
    4 I always do it
    5 Other

10. Who paid the charge for most of your searches? (Choose the *one* answer which best represents your experience.)

    1 I paid it out of my pocket
    2 It was charged to my grant
    3 Department paid it
    4 Library/institution paid it
    5 Partially out of my pocket; partially by other source
    6 Other (please specify): _____

11. How satisfied were you with the results of your most recent searches?

Very satisfied	Mildly satisfied	Neutral	Mildly unsatisfied	Very unsatisfied	Not sure
1	*2*	*3*	*4*	*5*	*6*

12. Some libraries have put some or all of their card catalog in a computer so that patrons may use a computer terminal to search for the books they want. Has part or all of the catalog in your institution's library been computerized? (If you use one of several libraries, answer for the library you use most.)

    1 Yes   *2* Probably yes   *3* Probably not   *4* No   *5* Don't know

IF YES: ↓

Have you had the opportunity to use the computerized catalog?

    1 Yes   *2* No

IF YES: ↓

Thus far has your library's present application of this technology:

	Significantly	*Moderately*	*A little*	*Not at all*	*Don't know*
Decreased your use of the card catalog?	*1*	*2*	*3*	*4*	*5*
Increased your access to scholarly materials?	*1*	*2*	*3*	*4*	*5*
Increased your productivity as a teacher?	*1*	*2*	*3*	*4*	*5*
Increased your research productivity?	*1*	*2*	*3*	*4*	*5*
Made the use of the library more enjoyable?	*1*	*2*	*3*	*4*	*5*

13. Has your university or organization provided an opportunity, such as a seminar or tutorial for you to learn about the new technical services available in the library?

    1 Yes   *2* No

14. If your institution is a college or university, is a library orientation or instruction program provided for:

	Yes	*No*	*Not sure*
Freshmen	*1*	*2*	*3*
Junior-senior students	*1*	*2*	*3*
Graduate students	*1*	*2*	*3*

◄ **All Respondents**

15. Listed below are various types of scholarly materials which you may or may not have used—read, browsed, copied, etc.—during the past year for *keeping up in your field, your teaching, or your research.* Please rate the importance to you of each of the following sources of such materials. (Do not include textbooks in answering this question.)

Importance during past year:	*Great importance*	*Moderate importance*	*Slight importance*	*No importance*	*Did not use*
Materials (books, journals, etc.) that were already in my personal library	*1*	*2*	*3*	*4*	*5*
Materials that I purchased during the past year	*1*	*2*	*3*	*4*	*5*
Colleagues' copies	*1*	*2*	*3*	*4*	*5*
Materials in my institution's library	*1*	*2*	*3*	*4*	*5*
Materials obtained through interlibrary loan	*1*	*2*	*3*	*4*	*5*
Materials identified through the use of computerized literature search	*1*	*2*	*3*	*4*	*5*

III. PROFESSIONAL READING

1. Including any scholarly journals you may receive as a benefit of membership in professional societies, how many scholarly journals do you currently subscribe to? (Do not count journals which publish only book reviews.) How many come from your membership(s)?

    Total paid subscriptions (including memberships) _____

    Number of above which you receive from professional society memberships _____

2. Is this the same number of journals you subscribed to during the preceding year, or have you increased or decreased the number of your subscriptions?

1 Same number   *2* Increase   *3* Decrease   *4* Currently have no subscriptions

IF DECREASE:

Which one of the following best describes why you decreased the number of your journal subscriptions?

1 Not enough time to read all the material I now receive
2 No longer interested in the field the journal(s) cover
3 Subscription price(s) was increased
4 Needed to cut my expenses
5 Other (please specify): _____

3. In addition to the journals you subscribe to, how many other scholarly journals in your or other fields do you *currently* monitor systematically (such as browsing through them to see if there are articles of interest to you)? (Enter zero if applicable.)

Examine each issue as it comes out.   Approximately _____ journals
Periodically (at least once a year) examine current issues.   Approximate y _____ journals

4. During the past year, have you read any of the following literary or scientific publications aimed at a broader audience:

	Yes regula ly	Yes occasionally	Yes once	No
The American Scholar	*1*	*2*	*3*	*4*
The Chronicle of Higher Education	*1*	*2*	*3*	*4*
Humanities (published by the National Endowment for the Humanities)	*1*	*2*	*3*	*4*
Science, Scientific American, Technology Today or Science 85	*1*	*2*	*3*	*4*
New York Times Book Review, Times Literary Supplement, New York Review of Books	*1*	*2*	*3*	*4*

5. During this past year approximately how many scholarly books (excluding textbooks) did you *purchase* from your own funds for your personal library?

Approximately _____ books, which included ____ ____ paperbacks

6. Please indicate your agreement or disagreement with each of the following statements about aspects of the scholarly publishing system.

	Strongly agree	Agree	Neutral	Disagree	Strongly disagree	No opinion
Even taking inflation into account, most scholarly books are very overpriced	*1*	*2*	*3*	*4*	*5*	*6*
It is virtually impossible to even minimally keep up with the literature in my field	*1*	*2*	*3*	*4*	*5*	*6*
When I look at a new issue of my discipline's major journal I rarely find an article that interests me	*1*	*2*	*3*	*4*	*5*	*6*
Most new books I want to read are reviewed quickly enough in the journals I read	*1*	*2*	*3*	*4*	*5*	*6*

7. Please make a rough estimate of the approximate total cost of the following to you during the past year.

	Total cost for past year:
Scholarly books I purchased.	Approximately $_____
Scholarly journals, including society dues for membership.	Approximately $_____

IV. RESEARCH AND PUBLICATION

1. Have you (with or without coauthors) ever published any of the following? If yes, please give the approximate total number that have appeared in print. (Please do *not* include items which have not yet appeared in print, even if they have been accepted for publication.)

	Ever published		Approximate
	Yes	*No*	*total number*
Textbook	*1*	*2*	_____
Scholarly book or monograph (editor or co-editor)	*1*	*2*	_____
Scholarly book or monograph (author or co-author)	*1*	*2*	_____
Chapter in a scholarly book	*1*	*2*	_____
Article in a refereed journal	*1*	*2*	_____
Comment in a refereed journal	*1*	*2*	_____
Book review in a scholarly journal	*1*	*2*	_____
Scholarly paper in conference proceedings	*1*	*2*	_____
Book review in newspaper or general magazine	*1*	*2*	_____
Short story, novel, or poetry	*1*	*2*	_____
Nonfiction essay/article/op ed piece in newspaper or general magazine	*1*	*2*	_____

2. Have you ever:

	Yes	*No*
Served as a referee for a scholarly journal article	*1*	*2*
Evaluated a scholarly book manuscript for a publisher	*1*	*2*
Served as an editor or associate editor of a scholarly journal	*1*	*2*
Distributed copies of your research papers before publication to other scholars in electronic form	*1*	*2*
Written a paper with a colleague using electronic mail or an electronic network to facilitate the collaboration	*1*	*2*
Received a research grant of $1,000 or more from an outside funding agency (e.g. foundation, National Science Foundation, etc.) since leaving graduate school (including grants to a team or group project)	*1*	*2*

3. How many people in your present department or organization:

	None	*One*	*Two*	*Three*	*Four*	*Five or more*
Do you regard as sharing one or more of your research interests?	*0*	*1*	*2*	*3*	*4*	*5*
Do you regularly ask to give comments on your draft scholarly manuscripts?	*0*	*1*	*2*	*3*	*4*	*5*
Have you co-authored a scholarly paper or publication with?	*0*	*1*	*2*	*3*	*4*	*5*

4. Outside your department, how many people at your institution or elsewhere:

	None	*One*	*Two*	*Three*	*Four*	*Five or more*
Do you regularly ask to give comments on your draft scholarly manuscripts?	*0*	*1*	*2*	*3*	*4*	*5*
Have you co-authored a scholarly paper or publication with?	*0*	*1*	*2*	*3*	*4*	*5*

5. How important to your teaching and research is the pre-publication material you receive from your colleagues?

1 More important than journal articles
2 As important as published journal articles
3 Useful, but less important than published journal articles
4 Of little or no importance
5 Do not receive such material

6. With regard to the last article you wrote which was accepted for publication in a refereed journal, how many journals was the article submitted to? (Put "0" if you have never submitted such an article.)

_____ Journals

7. How do you feel, overall, about the length of time it takes refereed journals to get your articles into print *once they have been accepted?*

    1 Very satisfied   *2* Satisfied   *3* Neutral   *4* Dissatisfied   *5* Very dissatisfied   *6* No opinion

8. Have you published all or part of your dissertation in the original or in a revised form (excluding microform copy for University Microfilm)?

    1 Published all or most as a book or monograph
    2 Published part of it as book or in an article(s)
    3 Published none of it
    4 Did not write a dissertation

9. How often, if at all, do you think the peer review refereeing system for scholarly journals in your field is biased *in favor* of the following categories of people?

	Rarely or never	In-frequently	Occa-sionally	Frequently	Not sure
Established researchers in a scholarly speciality	*1*	*2*	*3*	*4*	*5*
Scholars from prestigious institutions	*1*	*2*	*3*	*4*	*5*
Males	*1*	*2*	*3*	*4*	*5*
Whites					
Scholars who use currently fashionable approaches to a subject	*1*	*2*	*3*	*4*	*5*

10. Please give your opinion on the following statements about the scholarly publishing process.

	Strongly agree	Agree	Neutral	Disagree	Strongly disagree	No opinion
The number of journal outlets in my field is sufficient for my needs.	*1*	*2*	*3*	*4*	*5*	*6*
The number of publishers who publish books in my area of specialization is sufficient for my needs.	*1*	*2*	*3*	*4*	*5*	*6*
I feel I have enough information to decide where to submit scholarly *articles* for publication.	*1*	*2*	*3*	*4*	*5*	*6*
Faculty tenure committees should consider *refereed* material published in nontraditional forms (such as microform, publication "on demand," electronic journals, etc.) as comparable to material published in conventional forms.	*1*	*2*	*3*	*4*	*5*	*6*
The peer review system in my discipline needs reform	*1*	*2*	*3*	*4*	*5*	*6*

11. Have you ever supplied a book or article manuscript to a publisher direct from your computer in the form of a computer tape, diskette, or other machine readable form?

    1 Yes   *2* No   *3* Don't know, not sure

V. COMPUTER RESOURCES AND USE

1. Does the secretary who does your work, if you have one, use a wordprocessor to prepare your materials?

    1 Yes   *2* No   *3* Have no secretary

2. What is *your* level of skill in each of the following?

	Excellent	Good	Fair	Poor	None
Touch typing	*1*	*2*	*3*	*4*	*5*
Wordprocessing	*1*	*2*	*3*	*4*	*5*
Computer programming (any language)	*1*	*2*	*3*	*4*	*5*
Use of statistical analysis packages such as SAS or SPSS	*1*	*2*	*3*	*4*	*5*

3. What type (or types) of computers do you or your research assistant have access to, and which, if any, do you use? (Please circle the number for all categories below that apply.)

Note: "Access" means that a computer keyboard or terminal is available to you for communicating directly with the computer. It does not mean such things as sending course evaluation forms to a central campus location where someone else processes them on a computer.

	(A) Access			(B) Do you use currently?	
	Have access to	Unsure, may have access to	Do not have access to	Yes	No
Mainframe central computer for wordprocessing or computation	*1*	*2*	*3*	*1*	*2*
Minicomputer (such as a VAX) serving multiple users, for word-processing or computation	*1*	*2*	*3*	*1*	*2*
Dedicated wordprocessing system (such as Wang or NBI system) which serves one or more users	*1*	*2*	*3*	*1*	*2*
Microcomputer owned by you or by your institution (such as IBM Personal Computer, IBM PC/XT, Apple IIe, or MacIntosh) serving one or a few users	*1*	*2*	*3*	*1*	*2*

4. Do you or your research assistant (if you have one) personally use any computer in your research or teaching (including wordprocessing)? (Exclude library terminals used to access the card catalog.)

	Yes	No
You personally	*1*	*2*
Your research assistant	*1*	*2*

◄ **If you answered "yes" to either of these questions skip to question 7.**

5. *If you do not use a computer*, do you (or your assistant) have any current plans to use one?

    1 No   *2* Yes, intend to begin to use it this academic year
    3 Yes, intend to begin to use it sometime in the near future   *4* Not sure

6. Which one of the following reasons best describes why you have not yet begun to use a computer in your work? (Circle one number.)

    1 I don't feel it would be of any use to me
    2 It is more trouble than it is worth
    3 I don't have any access to a computer at my institution
    4 I find computers intimidating
    5 It costs too much to use the computer at my institution
    6 Location of computer is inconvenient
    7 Other (please describe): _____

◄ **Skip to question 23.**

7. What is the location of the closest computer or computer terminal of any kind (including your own) that you have access to at your institution?

    1 My office   *2* Nearby office   *3* Same building   *4* Library   *5* Other building

8. How often is this computer or terminal available for you to use when you want to?

   1 All the time   *2* Most of the time   *3* Sometimes   *4* Hardly ever   *5* Never   *6* Not sure

9. If you (or your assistant) *use* a computer—either your own or one belonging to your institution—thus far how important *to you* have been each of the following types of use?

	Very important	Somewhat important	Neutral	Somewhat unimportant	Very unimportant
General wordprocessing	*1*	*2*	*3*	*4*	*5*
Using my institution's on-line library card catalog	*1*	*2*	*3*	*4*	*5*
Accessing data bases through online service networks including searching bibliographic data bases	*1*	*2*	*3*	*4*	*5*
Electronic mail to communicate with colleagues in *other* institutions or campuses	*1*	*2*	*3*	*4*	*5*
Electronic mail to communicate with colleagues at *your* campus or institution	*1*	*2*	*3*	*4*	*5*
Compiling a bibliography or index	*1*	*2*	*3*	*4*	*5*
Maintaining note files for teaching, research, or other activities	*1*	*2*	*3*	*4*	*5*
Preparing a concordance, dictionary, thesaurus, critical edition, editing a collection of letters	*1*	*2*	*3*	*4*	*5*
Theme, text, semantic, or foreign language analysis	*1*	*2*	*3*	*4*	*5*
Statistical analysis of data	*1*	*2*	*3*	*4*	*5*
Helping students in my classes understand the material covered in my courses (computer-assisted teaching).	*1*	*2*	*3*	*4*	*5*
Test preparation	*1*	*2*	*3*	*4*	*5*
Grading tests or papers	*1*	*2*	*3*	*4*	*5*
Preparing budgets	*1*	*2*	*3*	*4*	*5*
Preparing charts, diagrams or computer graphics	*1*	*2*	*3*	*4*	*5*
Maintaining curriculum vitae	*1*	*2*	*3*	*4*	*5*

10. Considering all the uses you identified in the previous question, what proportion of the total computer use performed by you and your assistant on your behalf do you do personally?

   1 All   *2* Most   *3* Some   *4* Hardly any   *5* None   *6* Not sure

11. Do you *personally own* (or have on loan for your exclusive personal use) a personal (micro) computer or computer terminal which you use for your work either at home or at your institution?

	Personal computer	*Computer terminal*
Ownership	*1* Own	*1* Own
	2 Have on loan	*2* Have on loan
	3 Both	*2* Both
	4 Neither	*4* Neither
Place of use	*1* Use at home	*1* Use at home
	2 Use at office	*2* Use at office
	3 Use at both places	*3* Use at both places
	4 Do not have	*4* Do not have

◄ **If you do NOT own or have on loan a personal computer** *(not a terminal)* **which you use for your work skip to question 17.**

12. What year did you buy or obtain your computer? (If your current computer is not your first, please also give the year you bought the first computer you used for your work.)

   Current computer: 19___   First computer: 19___

13. What is the make/model of your current personal computer? (If you have more than one, list the most powerful one you personally own.)

   1 Apple IIe   *2* MacIntosh   *3* Osborne/Kaypro   *4* IBM PC   *5* IBM AT or XT

   6 IBM PC Compatible (e.g., Columbia, Compaq, etc.)   *7* Other (please specify): _____

14. Which of the following do you own or have on loan for your personal computer? Check as many as apply.

____ Database management/file/program (e.g., dBase II, PFS File)

____ Database/wordprocessing program specifically designed for scholars (e.g. Nota Bene)

____ Spread sheet program (e.g. VisiCalc)

____ Program that combines wordprocessing with spreadsheet and other capabilities (e.g. Lotus 1-2-3, Jazz etc.)

____ Separate wordprocessing program (e.g. WordStar)

____ Statistical analysis program

____ Modem

15. Can you currently transfer the wordprocessing or data analysis you do on your personal computer—personally owned or on loan—to your institution's system and vice versa (e.g., so you can print your documents on letter quality printers, send electronic mail etc)?

1 Yes *2* Yes, but with difficulty *3* No *4* Don't know, unsure

16. Which *two* factors were most important in causing you to purchase or obtain the first computer you listed in question 8 above? Place a 1 by the factor which was most important, and a 2 by the second most important factor.

Rank

_____ Needed it for consulting work

_____ Needed it to aid my teaching activities

_____ My institution gave it to me

_____ Purchased it primarily for the use of other family members

_____ I got a very good discount on it through my institution

_____ My general interest in computers

_____ Needed it to aid in scholarly writing activities

_____ Needed it to aid in scholarly research activities (apart from writing manuscripts)

17. During the past year what percentage of the total cost (computer time and data storage charges, purchase of hardware and software) for your computer use—including your own computer which you use for your work if you have one—was covered by each of the following:

_____ % Money from grants for projects you are working on

_____ % University/Department allocations and subsidies

_____ % Personal (including consulting income)

_____ % Other (please specify:) _____

100%

18. Overall, how satisfied are you with the software you currently use for the following purposes? (If you use different software for your personal computer and for an institutional computer which you also use, answer this question for your personal computer software.)

	Very satisfied	Satisfied	Neither	Un-satisfied	Very un-satisfied	Don't use
Wordprocessing	*1*	*2*	*3*	*4*	*5*	*6*
Statistical analysis	*1*	*2*	*3*	*4*	*5*	*6*
Database management	*1*	*2*	*3*	*4*	*5*	*6*
Grading and record keeping	*1*	*2*	*3*	*4*	*5*	*6*
Classroom teaching	*1*	*2*	*3*	*4*	*5*	*6*

19. Is there any software you would like to have for your teaching or research which is not currently available for purchase? If yes, please briefly describe your greatest software need on the back page of the questionnaire. This will facilitate our sharing your needs with software developers.

1 Yes *2* No

20. Have you ever written or are you currently writing a program for use in your:

Classes *1* Yes *2* No
Research *2* Yes *2* No

21. What are your biggest problems with using computers at your institution? (Circle *no more than two* items.)

   1 No particular problem
   2 Insufficient access to a terminal or computer
   3 Lack of particular hardware to do what I want to do
   4 Poor maintenance of hardware
   5 Lack of particular software to do what I want to do
   6 Lack of computer advice and assistance
   7 Printers not conveniently located
   8 Poor printer quality
   9 Insufficient training opportunities
  10 Difficulty of linking my computer with other computers at my institution
  11 Other (please specify:) _____

22. If you use any computer for research or writing, please give your best judgment about how this has improved or impaired the following aspects of your work by circling one position on this scale (skip any statements that do not apply):

Effect on:	Greatly improved	Improved	Slightly improved	Little or no effect	Slightly impaired	Impaired	Greatly impaired
My research productivity	1	2	3	4	5	6	7
My creativity in examining my research data in new ways	1	2	3	4	5	6	7
The overall quality of my research	1	2	3	4	5	6	7
My writing efficiency	1	2	3	4	5	6	7
The quality of my writing	1	2	3	4	5	6	7
The quality of my teaching	1	2	3	4	5	6	7
My enjoyment of my work as a scholar	1	2	3	4	5	6	7

23. How much experience did you have in using computers when you were a graduate student?

  1 Great deal   *2* Fair amount   *3* Some   *4* A little   *5* None

24. If you work at an academic institution, how strong is your *institution's* current encouragement of undergraduate use of computers?

  1 Very strong   *2* Strong   *3* Moderate   *4* Weak   *5* Very weak   *6* Not sure

25. All things considered, do you think computers will have a positive, negative, or neutral effect on the intellectual progress of *your discipline* in the next five years?

  1 Very positive   *2* Positive   *3* Neutral   *4* Negative   *5* Very negative   *6* Don't know, not sure

26. All things considered, do you think computers will have a positive, negative, or neutral effect on how your discipline is *taught* to undergraduate and graduate students in the next five years?

  1 Very positive   *2* Positive   *3* Neutral   *4* Negative   *5* Very negative   *6* Don't know, not sure

SUPPLEMENTAL INFORMATION

1. In what year were you born?   19__

2. Are you?   *1* Male   *2* Female

3. Are you?   *1* White   *2* Black   *3* Mexican-American, Hispanic-American
   4 Asian-American   *5* Other

4. Please circle the number on the list below which best represents your estimated *total* household income from all sources in 1985 *before taxes.*

  1 Below $15,000   *3* $20,000 – $24,999   *5* $30,000 – $34,999   *7* $40,000 – $49,999   *9* $65,000 – $80,000
  2 $15,000 – $19,999   *4* $25,000 – $29,999   *6* $35,000 – $39,999   *8* $50,000 – $64,999 *10* Over $80,000

5. How many people in your household will earn more than $5,000 in 1985?

  1 One   *2* Two   *3* Three or more

6. In the last three years have you done consulting work for pay?

  1 No
  2 Yes, earning an average of $1,000 or less per year
  3 Yes, earning an average of more than $1,000 per year

7. Graduate departments are often ranked on the basis of the scholarly attainments of their faculty and graduates, If you teach in a department which awards the Ph.D., which of the following best fits the *current* rank of your department?

  1 Among the top 5 departments in your discipline
  2 Among the top 10 departments in your discipline
  3 Among the top 20 departments in your discipline
  4 Among the top 30 departments in your discipline
  5 Among the top 40 departments in your discipline
  6 Not sure

The following questions will provide useful information but are strictly optional. None of the results of this questionnaire will be reported in such a way that individuals may be identified and all results will be confidential.

8. What is the name of the institution where you are currently employed?

  _____

9. Where is this institution located?

  State: _____ Town/City: _____

Thank you for completing the questionnaire. Please return it in the enclosed stamped envelope to:
Survey of Scholars
c/o Action Surveys, Inc.
7564 Standish Place
Rockville, Md 20855

Also please return the stamped postcard.

Comments on software (continuation of question 19, page 11):

Other comments:

IV. Special Analysis

Marketing, User Surveys, and the Library in Transition

Paul B. Kantor, Tantalus Inc

The Library in Transition

The present era is one in which libraries are "in transition."[1] In fact, one wonders whether they will ever return to a comfortable stability in structure and function, matching the one that has persisted since the time of Alexandria. Computers and telecommunication are transforming the methods of internal records management, the scope and means of library access, and even the "stuff itself"—the monographs and periodicals in which knowledge is stored. The end of this transition is surely not in sight.

The potential of interlibrary lending

For the library in transition, access to resources does not simply mean purchase or subscription. It also includes interlibrary lending, supported by electronic searching. The late Hugh Atkinson, University Librarian at the University of Illinois, defined the borrowing aspect of the problem this way[2]:

> A library will borrow in its areas of strength, rather than in its areas of weakness, because those are the areas that its users need. It is known[3] that about one of every three requests for library material is frustrated because the material is not available. It should be possible to fill one third of those frustrated requests by borrowing from other institutions, either large or small. The result is that interlibrary borrowing should be equal to about one tenth of total circulation.

The statistics compiled by the Association of Research Libraries (ARL) cannot tell us how far interlibrary resource shar-

1. Warren J. Haas, President of the Council on Library Resources, coined this phrase. The sense is outlined in his introduction to *The Economics of Research Libraries,* by Martin M. Cummings. Washington, D.C. Council on Library Resources, 1986.
2. Personal communication to Paul B. Kantor.
3. The techniques which establish this type of information are laid out in "Objective Measures for academic and Research Libraries" by Paul B. Kantor. Available from the Association of Research Libraries.

ing is from Atkinson's target, because they report interlibrary activity but do not report total circulation. We can see, however, that for the university libraries in the ARL, total borrowing is 865,000 items and total budget is $946 million (1984 –85 statistics.[4]) That is, about one item borrowed for each thousand dollars of total expenditure. Interlibrary borrowing is clearly a tiny part of the picture. But at the University of Illinois the corresponding figure is 132,000 items borrowed and the budget is $14 million. The ratio is nearly ten times as large (9.4 items borrowed per thousand dollars.) Thus ARL statistics suggest that, roughly speaking, interlibrary borrowing is 9 times more of a factor in access for scholars at the University of Illinois than it is at the average ARL library.

But this is not because of weakness in the collection. The ratio of holding to dollars at Illinois is 6.8 million volumes to $14.4 or about .5 volumes per dollar. The corresponding ratio for all libraries combined is .28 volumes per dollar. Hence, the collection at Illinois is larger, compared to the budget, than it is at the average ARL library. (Correspondingly, if ILL borrowing were compared to holdings, it would be 4.5 times as important at Illinois as at the average ARL university library.) Budget is the preferred base, because that indicates what the university spends to obtain access to scholarly materials. Holdings represent the past investment.

New modes of access

In a provocative essay appearing in the January 1987 issue of *Library Resources and Technical Services,* Jay David Bolter suggests that the electronic storage and transmission of information is a landmark in the communication of human thought, ranking with the invention of the papyrus, the codex, and the printing press. He suggests that the very ways in which we think of and combine information will be transformed to exploit the potential of the electronic medium. The most obvious advantage is the ease

4. Daval, Nicola and A. Lichtenstein. *ARL Statistics: 1984–85.* Washington D.C. 1986 Association of Research Libraries. Obviously, dividing anything by the total budget is only a very rough measure of performance. More detailed description would involve functional cost analysis, in which all of the costs in that total budget are allocated to specific activities and functions. Details are given in the FUNCOST package of software for IBM-PC compatible computers, available from Tantalus Inc.

with which an entire text can be searched to finds words, or word combinations of interest. The library of 25 years from now will support a different kind of access to a different kind of knowledge. For the humanist, primary texts in Greek and French are becoming available in this form. The technical problems of retrospectively storing and indexing a printed book in computer format are probably solvable within the decade.

Distributed Scholarship

Dr. Larry Smarr, head of the Supercomputer Center, coincidentally, also at the University of Illinois, has pointed out that the combined computing power of the microcomputers on desks around the country already exceeds the combined power of all the Cray and Cyber supercomputers combined.

In precisely the same way, humanistic scholarship can and should flourish in small centers, as well as in a few super schools. Most humanists want and need to teach, which requires access to students. Scholars draw, from those students, renewed enthusiasm for the topics of importance. The key ingredients for distributed scholarship are good communication and excellent access to resources. Scholars at liberal arts colleges already are substantial borrowers of materials from other centers, and are accustomed to looking beyond their own campuses for library support.

Just as there are super-computers, there are super-libraries. One of the striking results of the Survey of Scholars is that scholars at research institutions are overwhelmingly more pleased with the services of their libraries than are scholars at other types of institutions. This effect is much stronger than the correlation between pleasure with the library and general "job satisfaction." It must be concluded that these scholars enjoy, quite literally, the better access to needed materials.

If electronic communication can improve the access for scholars located elsewhere, there can be a substantial flourishing in humanistic scholarship without the impossible expense of duplicating the nation's 110 giant research libraries at every scholar's doorstep.

The key ingredient here is a recognition, by the research libraries, by networks such as OCLC and RLIN, and by catalytic organizations such as the Council on Library Resources, that "research libraries" could have a broader meaning—encompassing any and all libraries that are used to support research.

From this perspective, what are often called "college libraries" are also, part of the time, "research libraries." Not large enough to join the club, but important enough to merit support, both public and private, to improve their service to scholars.

The Library Marketing Problem

Librarians have long recognized the need to know more about what scholars want and how well they are served. Most studies have been limited to single libraries. Usually they have too much detail about the library and too little detail about the scholars. The studies are also more likely to include those who do use the library than those who don't.

Selling versus marketing

The Council on Library Resources' third seminar on the Economics of Academic Libraries identified marketing knowledge as a key need for libraries in transition. In the common language, marketing is often confused with "selling." Of course, libraries do not sell their services. But marketing refers to studying the market that one serves, to determine its needs and preferences. This is particularly important when there is no price mechanism to tell librarians whether they are really doing what is needed. Each academic or research library deals with, for the most part, a captive population of clients or users. The growth of service to this population must be informed by studies of their needs and preferences.

If you wanted to know, why didn't you ask?

In an important address to the Association of Research Libraries, in May 1986, Dr. William Hubbard summarized the problem this way.

> "One way to find out what the user needs are—and I do not mean to be glib—is to ask them. There have been some very provocative studies ...in which library users were asked to rank in order of their preference the various functional programs of the library. These studies are available in the literature; they are not very sophisticated or satisfying.
>
> You look at the trends of what users are actually doing and then ask yourself whether there is an activity that has an economically effective component. I believe one's own objectives are derived from one's image of what serves best."

A careful review of literature reveals that more than 80 articles or reports have been published on the problem of the needs of library users during the past few years. Ninety percent of these discussions lack specific data and conclusions about the needs of scholars. However, several articles help to set the stage for understanding the present report. In Supplement A, we touch briefly on the high points of those studies that report data on faculty perceptions of the library.

Analyzing the results

The key problem in analyzing the results of any such library surveys is two fold.

1. The data naturally present themselves in tables showing what percentage of this type of user do or do not like that type of library service. But what we need to know is comparative data. Is the response of one user group significantly different from another?

2. Perhaps more importantly, is the response at this particular library significantly different from what would be expected at any library in the country? The first question is important in linking library performance to the institution's profile of goals and strengths. The second is important in assessing how well the library compares to those at peer institutions.

The Need for a Standard Instrument

A standard survey instrument for looking at the needs of scholars, and at the adequacy of the library, is a necessary first step beyond the present, unsatisfactory situation. The study by the Office of Scholarly Communication and Technology provides a questionnaire that can serve that purpose. At the same time, the results of the survey teach us three important lessons.

• Humanists will respond, at a high (over 70%) level, to an in-depth survey about their information needs, scholarly activities, and appraisal of the library. (The 16-page questionnaire required 30–40 minutes to complete.)

• There are many significant correlations of scholars' evaluation of the library with other important variables describng their "external scholarly activity" and their situational characteristics such as discipline, age, rank, quality of the department or the institution, and so on.

• Colleges and universities can draw on the survey results to rethink the needs of their own scholars and, most importantly, *they can replicate the study, or parts of it, locally, to get precise information for planning and evaluation.*

Scope of the study

The questionnaire, as explained earlier, was mailed to more than 5,000 humanists, drawn from the membership of eight scholarly societies. The overall response rate was 71 percent. Because the study was aimed in part at understanding the views and needs of the member societies, the number of respondents from each society was about the same, although the size of the societies, and the corresponding disciplines, varies considerably. The questionnaire was divided into five parts as follows: Personal and Institutional Background, Library Resources, Professional Reading, Research and Publication, Computer Resources and Use.

In the Survey of Scholars the number of respondents in each discipline was large enough to permit extensive cross tabulation at a level where statistically significant relations may emerge.

The special analysis of library issues

The data gathered ranged over a variety of topics. For purposes of the analysis described below the most important are library variables, situational variables, and internal scholarly activity variables.

Library variables are reflected in responses to statements such as: "Rate the adequacy of journal holdings for my specialized research needs." The alternatives were "Excellent, very good, good, fair, poor and not sure."

To clarify the analysis we have recoded all such variables into two groups: Favorable (Excellent, Very Good) and Unfavorable (Poor, Fair). In other words, we have not tried to interpret responses such as "not sure" and we have excluded the response in the center of the scale. This deals realistically with the common situation in which responses are distributed in the proportions:

Low	Next	Good	Next	High
10	10	70	10	0.

Such a distribution may be summarized as "80 percent rated the library at Good or better." It seems more important to note that of those who had a "noncentral" opinion, twice as many gave low scores.

Situational variables include sex, discipline, characteristics of the institution, job satisfaction, and so on. Where appropriate, these have been recoded by the same process used for the library variables. When the variable has several values which do not lend themselves to interpretation on an ordered scale, we have recoded them into each versus all others. For example, we created a variable DISC1 representing English (= 1) and all the other disciplines (= 2). This makes it possible to contrast each discipline separately with all of the others combined. Since the number for all of the others combined represents members of several societies, the data are weighted to represent the sizes of the societies.

External scholarly activity variables include publishing, attending conferences, chairing sessions, and so on. It may be important to know whether the library is serving these scholars as well as they expect. Since such outside activities bring them in contact with other scholars, it is likely that their expectations will reflect the situation at other institutions. It was shown, in a preliminary investigation not reported here, that scholars scoring high on any measures of external scholarly activity tend to score high on others. Thus they represent a well-defined group whose needs are of special interest to colleges and universities. They are most likely to be the "distributed scholars" discussed above.

Technique of analysis

The survey data have been analyzed by a very powerful technique called cross-product ratio analysis (XPR analysis). This analysis takes a table with four numbers in it, and sums it up in a single ratio.

For example, we find that the relation between scholars in literature and other scholars, when asked to evaluate the *adequacy of library journal holdings for their research,* is:

	SCHOLARS IN LITERATURE	OTHERS
FAVORABLE	185	982
UNFAVORABLE	199	833

We can see that literary scholars seem more inclined to give an unfavorable score to the library than do other scholars. The XPR makes this relation precise by calculating a ratio of ratios:

$$\frac{\text{LITERATURE (FAVORABLE vs UNFAVORABLE)}}{\text{OTHERS (FAVORABLE vs UNFAVORABLE)}} = \frac{185/199}{982/833}$$

$$= (185 \times 833)/(199 \times 983)$$

$$= 0.79$$

Standard statistical methods[5] tell us that this result is statistically significant at more than 95 percent confidence. We can put it in words by saying "Scholars in literature are only 79 percent as likely to be pleased with library journal holdings, for research, as are other scholars."

Comments on the technique

The XPR technique has two important benefits. One is clarity. A set of four numbers, whose specific values are determined in part by sample design and response rate, is reduced to a single figure, focussed on differentiating response by group. The second is resistance to bias. The cross product ratio is independent of many sampling effects, and so frees us from the need to sample all classes of respondents in fixed proportion. [The reader may verify that if the numbers in any row, or any column of the table are, for example, doubled, the XPR remains the same!]

We pay a price for these benefits. The XPR analysis applies only to pairwise comparisons—two values of one variable compared with two values of another. A typical result from the Survey of Scholars is a 5×7 cross-tabulation of responses by society. We have approached the two variables in different ways.

For responses which are perceived to represent a continuum we have concentrated on the outer ends, as described above. This is an enhancement technique, similar to the use of noise filters in video or audio equipment. The "noise" in this case is the set of responses lying exactly in the middle of the scale. Without extensive follow-up interviews we cannot know whether

5. The XPR measure is discussed in detail by Joseph Fleiss in *Statistical Methods for Ratios and Proportions* Wiley. 1981. The post-processor programs which determine the XPR from standard SPSSX crosstabulation output were developed at Tantalus by Paul Kantor and H. Altay Guvenir.

these responses represent a carefully measured judgement, benign disinterest, or some other mental state.

External scholarly activity also forms a continuum. For the corresponding variables (such as number of articles published) we have used the median for each variable to divide the respondents into the "Active" group and the "Others." This does not mean that the others are "inactive," but is merely a convenient way of describing the two groups. It seems unlikely, although we have no statistical evidence, that the respondent group contains much in the way of academic deadwood.

Discipline and type of institution represent categorical variables. There is no natural order or underlying continuum. We approached this problem by asking how libraries and institutions might use the survey results *for library planning*. Colleges and universities set goals, and evaluate standings in terms of disciplines, and identify certain disciplines as representing areas of strength, growth, or other concern. With this in mind we recoded the data so that for any particular discipline we may ask: "Does the library appear to serve this discipline as well as it serves all the others."

In defining "all the other disciplines" certain weight factors are used to adjust from the representation of each society in the sample to the total membership of the society. Thus, although classicists and literary scholars are about equally represented in the sample, the weight of the former group, in defining an overall sum, will be smaller. The overall normalization of the weight factors was chosen to reflect the actual number of respondents. While this has no effect on the cross product ratio, it is the necessary choice if we are to assess the statistical significance (t-value) of the results.

Two more examples are given below.

Another cross-product ratio analysis shows that sociologists are 39 percent more likely than other scholars to be pleased with the *adequacy of library journals for their research*. The remaining disciplines are not significantly different from each other (literally, from all but themselves.)

On the other hand, when appraising the *adequacy of book holdings for their own teaching needs*, the sociologists give the library low marks: there are only 74 percent as likely to be pleased as are the scholars in other fields. This result is also significant at better than the 95 percent confidence limit. In this case the countering group, which is more pleased than others, with the library, is composed of classicists.

A Sampling of Findings

A detailed analysis of nearly 600 potentially interesting correlations has yielded a wealth (several hundred) that are statistically significant. We do not have space to explore them all, but we have summarized some illustrative findings in exhibit 1. For pre-

Exhibit 1. *Adequacy of journal holdings for research needs*
(Groups that rate library holdings significantly favorable or significantly unfavorable compared to all other groups)

Types of scholars giving significantly high ratings	**Types of scholars giving significantly low ratings**
Sociologists	English scholars
Scholars in extremely selective institutions	All others
Men	Women
Full professors, lecturers	Others
Tenured	Tenure track (no tenure)
Teach equal mix of grad/undergraduates	Other combinations
Very satisfied with job	Other possibilities

Types of institutions where ratings are significantly high	**Types of institutions where ratings are significantly low**
Public	Private
Research institutions	Others
Institution offers PhD	Does not offer PhD

Degree of external scholarly activity

Above median	**Publish texts**	Below median
Above median	**Write articles**	Below median
Above median	**Write chapters**	Below median
Above median	**Write papers**	Below median
Above median	**Write fiction**	Below median

cise interpretation, each significant relationship should be interpreted by looking to the cross tabulation table to see which group has the more favorable attitude.

We give a few examples here to show how the interpretation works. In Table I, Part 7 (page 134 in this report) we find, for LDATAB (Access to computerized bibliographic databases) that GRAD (Primarily graduate teaching) has the following entry:

LDATAB GRAD   2.00   0.69   0.28   2.94   324*

The first number, the cross-product ratio, tells us that respondents in the group who primarily do graduate teaching are twice as likely to evaluate the access to databases as "Excellent" or "Very Good" (as against "Fair" or "Poor") as are the other scholars. The next two numbers are the logarithm of the ratio and the standard error, which are used in the statistical analysis, and their ratio .69/.28 = 2.64 is related to the t-value of the statistic. The true t-value is somewhat different (2.94) and is reported also. The number 324 refers to a page in the full output, and the asterisk indicates that the result is statistically significant.

Other variables having a strong relationship to the same aspect of library service are INTDS (Interdisciplinary) and INSTRUC (Instructor.)

| LDATAB | INSTRUC | 0.53 | -6.04 | 0.29 | -2.06 | 209* |
| LDATAB | INTDSC | 1.44 | 0.37 | 0.18 | 2.18 | 67* |

That is, instructors are just over half as likely to rate database access as excellent or good, whereas scholars in interdisciplinary research are almost half again more likely to give those ratings. This, like many of the other findings in the detailed tables, suggests that scholars' evaluations of the library may be greatly influenced by whether their own activities have moved them to seek out the resources that the library has to offer. Again, further research is needed on this point.

Some caveats

An important caveat must be mentioned before we scan a few highlights. It is quite likely that the "explanatory variables" are confounded. For example, scholars at research institutions are quite likely to be more active outside the institutions, to be more satisfied with their jobs, to be men rather than women, and so on. Thus, we cannot unravel the possible causative factors to say that every one of them is or is not a significant indicator of satisfaction with the library.

Further, we do not know whether it is the nature of the library that causes satisfaction, or whether it is something in the nature of the respondent. Perhaps people who are satisfied with their jobs are more likely to be satisfied about everything, including the library. A much more detailed analysis would be required to extract all of the useful information that is contained in the OSCT data tapes on these and other questions.

Summary observations

We have reviewed the hundreds of cross product ratio analyses to search for general patterns that may be easily summarized. For many of the observations which follow, the alert reader will have no difficulty supplying a "likely explanation." *However, the assertions are made here not because they seem likely, but because they appear with statistical significance, in the data.* The reader is encouraged to search for "likely explanations" of the opposite conclusions as well. It is when both the result and its opposite are plausible that the data are really providing critical evidence.

In what follows we are forced to speak of the scholars' "satisfaction" with the library because the Survey of Scholars asked only for opinions, and not for concrete experiences.

Generally speaking, scholars who are more satisfied with their "careers" are more satisfied with every aspect of the library. Those at larger, higher ranking, more selective institutions are more satisfied with the library. Scholars at Research institutions, and those at PhD-granting institutions are satisfied with all services except online searching. In contrast, scholars at all other institutions are less satisfied with all services except that one. As mentioned above, these may be the same scholars, identifying themselves by another trait. For example, scholars at institutions offering the PhD are no doubt at the larger institutions.

Literary scholars are generally less satisfied with the library than are others. Scholars who are more than usually active outside the institution are generally more satisfied with service. The exception is those scholars who write fiction—they are generally less satisfied with the library.

Scholars in all intermediate ranks tend to be unsatisfied with the library. The exceptions are full professors and lecturers. This is a significant finding, as the full unsatisfied group includes the assistant and associate professors whose work is the arrow of the future. It suggests that the library is viewed most critically by those struggling for tenure, and is significant for academic administrators, concerned with attracting and holding the best scholars.

Findings such as these pose important questions for further research. For example, why does the same collection leave some scholars satisfied and others dissatisfied. Is it due to the nature of the library's holdings, or services? Is it, perhaps, due to differences in the scholars' personal collections, or to the peer group norms which they adopt?

Scholars at public institutions are more satisfied with research adequacy of journals. Those at private institutions are more satisfied with availability of trained reference librarians. It is interesting to know whether this correlates with any differences in staffing pattern at the two types of institutions. For example, it may be that public institutions make more use of student assistants and other apprentices in the reference role.

Scholars at more highly selective institutions are more satisfied with the library generally. Note that this is not a simple replicate of the finding in favor of research institutions, as some of the most selective undergraduate institutions are colleges.

Male scholars are more satisfied than female. This is a good example of the "confounding of variables" problem. Detailed study is needed to determine whether this result is what one would expect from the fact that women are disproportionately represented in the lower ranks, which we already know to be dissatisfied. Again, this is an area for further research.

Scholars who teach an equal mix of graduate and undergraduate are most satisfied with the library. Those who teach only undergraduates are least satisfied. Those who are tenured are more satisfied than those who are not, but, as noted above, those who are tenure track, but not yet tenured, are least satisfied.

Implications for the Future

Both libraries and their host institutions have long struggled with the idiosyncracies of library studies. Each college or university reinvents the wheel, with so much local variation that it is hard to evaluate the results. Now each institution can, and should, include standard blocks of questions on the library, on situation, and on external scholarly activity. Since baseline statistics are available on all of these questions, the results can be interpreted in context, rather than in a vacuum.

There is an even more important prospect. The data tape prepared from questionnaires returned by survey scholars, and the analysis programs, can be made available so that new questions can be addressed to it. For example, a college may find that its faculty with heavy teaching loads are more dissatisfied with the library than are their colleagues. But we may wonder whether this is simply a reflection of overall dissatisfaction. We can construct the appropriate statistical table for the local data and also *address the same question to the Scholarly Communication Survey data tape*. In this way, we not only measure the local situation.

We can also say whether it is the same as, or different from, the situation elsewhere in the country.

The usefulness, to managers and administrators, of user surveys has taken a giant leap forward, as a result of this major study by the Office of Scholarly Communication and Technology. Computer tapes containing the survey data, and the programs that have been developed by Tantalus Inc can be used to substantially enhance the value of local surveys.

Organizations such as the Association of Research Libraries and the Council on Library Resources could provide, through kits, workshops and consultants, guidance on what questions to ask, and how to interpret the results.

With modest ongoing support from foundations such as the National Endowment for the Humanities, the humanist scholar could see his or her needs identified with a new level of objectivity, and correspondingly greater impact on those who manage the library and the college or university.

Such research can, and should complement the major efforts being made to harness new technology during this transition period. The Research Libraries Group has undertaken extensive studies of its combined holdings (the Conspectus Project.) The major online networks for access to library holdings (the RLIN, OCLC and WLN systems) are working towards links that are transparent to the users. When these two tasks are completed, the nations scholars will be able to draw on the enormous combined assets of the nation's academic and research libraries.

In this context, colleges and universities can aggressively monitor the needs of their own scholars, and the adequacy of their own library service to meet those needs. It is particularly important to identify and target the needs of humanist scholars early in the process, lest they become an under-served group at the library of the future. The ambitious survey by the Office of Scholarly Communication has shown us how it can be done. Now it is up to the libraries of our nation to show that it will be done.

Acknowledgements

The literature on library user studies was reviewed by Dr. Donna Trivison. The XPR post-processor was written in C-language by H. Altay Guvenir. Extensive analysis of the interrelation of variables indicating External Scholarly activity was carried out by Moula Cherikh. The author thanks Herbert Morton of the Office of Scholarly Communication and Technology for a thoughtful review of a draft version of this report, and many insightful suggestions.

Supplement A. Notes on library user studies

• Southwick studied faculty support towards the learning resources center at Ricks College (1983; N = 155 of 260). Sixty percent of the respondents judged that the resource center was adequate for their teaching needs frequently or very frequently, while only 21% judged it to be that adequate for their research needs. The media collection was most heavily used (54%) and the government documents collection least used; 64% of the faculty seek help from a librarian "frequently" and 83% report that the help is frequently of high quality.

• Jax did an awareness and user needs assessment at the University of Wisconsin-Stout Library Learning Center (1983: N = 224 of 524). The mean level of use reported by faculty is one visit per week. The major reasons for use are to borrow material and to use the reference service. Only 1.3% of the faculty report that they never use the library; 27% of the faculty report that all of the courses they teach require library use. The services reported as most useful were reference and audio-visual checkout (average rating 3.2 on a scale of 1 to 5). The services reported to be most valuable were reference (4.4), interlibrary loan, library instruction, the automated circulation system and AV checkout (all at 4.1); 33% of the faculty felt that the library should be open a greater number of hours; 29% would like to see the reference service available for longer periods, and 38% would like to see the loan period changed. With regard to collection adequacy, 69% of the respondents judged that 31 to 80% of what they need could be found in the library; 13% judged that less than 20% of what they needed could be found; 47% of the respondents used the interlibrary loan service. When asked to establish the relative value of various parts of the collection, 43% of the scholars cited the main circulation collection, while only 14% put the periodicals or the reference service first.

• D'Elia and others studied the document delivery service provided at the Twin Cities Campus of the University of Minnesota (1984; 99 of 155 users; 425 of 1006 nonusers). The focus of the study was to determine reasons for nonuse of the library. The reasons for use of document delivery were primarily the saving of time and reduction in effort. The most important for nonuse as measured by correlation were that the document can more easily be obtained from a colleague or the scholar lacked a specific citation. This study differs from others in that it did not simply report the user's perception of reason for nonuse, but concentrated on those perceptions which were positively correlated with the actual level of use (or nonuse).

With the collaboration of Donna Trevison

• Prather and others from the Georgia State University reported on a study of the assessment of a metropolitan university library by its users. (Winter, year not stated; 95 faculty in 3356 responses from 6157 questionnaires distributed in the library.) Faculty reasons for use were approximately evenly divided among books, magazines and others; 59% were using the library for their work as faculty members while 24% cited personal research as the reason for the visit; 55% reported that they use the library weekly; 74% reported that the library met most of their needs, while none reported that their needs were seldom met.

• Neal and Smith, at the Pennsylvania State University, surveyed 94 published authors (publications in 1979 or 1980) on the faculty (N = 83 or 94). Estimates of the percentage of needed materials for research that were obtained from the Penn State libraries were quite uniformly distributed from 0 to 100%; 53 authors provided information on the sources of material that they used. The most common responses were materials in their personal collections and/or materials borrowed from the libraries; 44 offered reasons for nonuse of the libraries. The most important reason given is that other libraries were more convenient. Some respondents suggested that document delivery was cumbersome or inconvenient. A further reason for nonuse was the absence of needed materials in the collection.

• Whitlatch studied library use patterns among full-time and part-time faculty and students at San Jose State University (N = 443 of 1753 surveyed by mail). Responses were analyzed with regard to respondent's teaching time, teaching load, sex, type of appointment and faculty discipline. Nonusers constituted 15.6% of the tenured faculty and 45.4% of the temporary faculty. Frequent users were 44% of the tenured track faculty and only 20% of the evening class faculty. Nonusers ranged from a low of 12% in social sciences to a high of 46% in the business faculty. Frequent users ranged from a high of 51% in the social science to a low of 20% in education. Of the humanities faculty, 18% characterized themselves as nonusers and 31% as frequent users. The primary reasons for nonuse of the library were greater convenience of another library (38%) and lack of time (23%). The faculty perception of the most important directions for allocation of library resources were the ordering of new books (56%), security of existing materials (52%), periodical subscriptions (45%), and better organization and shelving (43%).

• Frost studied student and faculty subject searching in an online public catalog (1985: N = 112 of 287) at the M.D. Anderson Library of the University of Houston. Of the respondents, 37% were in humanities or fine arts and another 37% in the social sciences; 62% reported that they use the library once a week or more, while only

13% reported that they used it less than once a month; 85% used the card catalog frequently or occasionally and 82% used the online catalog; 18% reported that they rarely or never used the online catalog. Among the users of the card catalog, the heaviest use is in humanities or fine arts (65% using it frequently) with business administration next and the social sciences reporting 42%. Frequent users of the card catalog did not frequently use the online catalog and vice versa. A large percentage (46%) indicated that they would use subject searching for interdisciplinary research; 40% used subject searching to update publications in their own area of specialization; 61% of the full professors (as compared with 40% of the associate professors and 33% of the assistant professors) used subject searches in this way.

• McCandless and others studied user needs for the University of Illinois Library. The goal was to determine whether users of computer-based systems have significant different needs and expectations than people who do not use those systems (1984: N = 615 of 1200 stratified sample of teaching faculty; 108 respondents to an online version of the questionnaire and two main frame systems). Of the respondents, 197 were social science faculty and 163 were humanities faculty. The sources of information mentioned most frequently by humanities faculty were their own books (91%), the card catalog (91.5%), and bibliographies or references in books and journals (89%). Online data bases were cited by only 16% of the users. When asked to evaluate enhancements that would improve service as provided by the LCS (the University of Illinois On-Line Access System), humanists gave top rank to increased number of terminals in disperse locations and second rank to training that would permit them to do their own online data base searches. Social scientists concurred in the first alternative but gave second rank to improved dial-up access to LCS, suggesting that more of the social scientists use micro computers or computer terminals on a frequent basis. Interestingly, scientists and social scientists had the same first three preferences with only the order changed. Natural scientists gave dial-ups first priority and an increased number of terminals third priority. When responses were analyzed according to the means by which the questionnaire was delivered, without regard to discipline, training to do online data base searching was ranked first by those who responded to the mail questionnaire, while more dial-ups, and 24-hour online reference service were ranked first by those who responded to the electronic questionnaire. Although this study focused only on access to bibliographic information, it does provide an important picture of the transformation occurring in the scholarly population.

• Link and others studied nonusers at the Michigan State University libraries (N = 211 of 405, 1984). The faculty sample was approximately at 10% stratified sample. The interview was conducted by telephone. Of the respondents, 24% reported that they rarely or never go to the library; 30% rarely or never asked for help, and 75% rarely or never phoned. The helpfulness of services provided at various points by those who were in a position to evaluate them ranged from a high of 92% for telephone services to 73% at the reference desk and 61% at the information desk. The primary faculty use of the library was to check out materials (84%), read current materials (76%), or obtain reference assistance (79%). Computer search was reported by 51% of the faculty. The key discouragement to library use (65%) was "too many demands on time." This was followed in a distant second by parking (41%), missing materials (40%), and inadequacy of library materials (38%). These authors also examined the correlation between library use and various factors such as the services principally used, expectations of the students or of the library and indicated discouragements. The authors were unable to determine whether perceptions determined degree of use or degree of use determined perceptions.

References

D'Elia, George and Others. *Evaluation of the Document Delivery Service Provided by University Libraries, Twin Cities Campus, University of Minnesota.* Final Report of a Research Project. ED 252 241. Minneapolis: University of Minnesota, May 1984, 62 pp.

Jane Dodd, Charles Gilreath, Geraldine Hutchins. *A Comparison of Two End-User Operated Search Systems.* Final Report, Sterling C. Evans Library, Texas A&M University. Office of Management Studies, Association of Research Libraries, Washington, D.C., January 1985

Frost, Carolyn O. *Student and Faculty Subject Searching in a University Online Public Catalog.* ED 264 872. Washington: Council on Library Resources, Inc., August 1985, 48 pp.

Jax, John J. *Library Awareness/User/Needs Assessment.* Parts I, II, and III. Ed 246 904. Wisconsin Univ. Stout, Menomonie: University of Wisconsin, January 1984, 149 pp.

Link, Terry, Kriss Ostrom, Agnes Haigh, Philip Marcus. *Nonusers of the MSU Libraries: An Assessment of Characteristics, Perceptions, and Needs at Michigan State University.* Michigan State University Library. Washington, D.C., Office of Management Studies, Association of Research Libraries, December 1984

McCandless, Patricia and Others. *The Invisible User: User Needs Assessment for Library Public Services.* Final Report from the Public Services Research Projects. ED 255 227. Urbana: University of Illinois Library, January 1985, 63 pp.

Neal, James G., Barbara J. Smith. "Library Support of Faculty Research at the Branch Campuses of a Multi-Campus University," *Journal of Academic Librarianship*, 9 (5) November 1983, 276–80

Prather, James E., Ralph E. Russell, Michael L. Clemons. "Library Resources of a Metropolitan University—Assessment by Users," *College & Research Libraries,* 44 (1) January 1983, 59-65

Southwick, Neal S. An Examination of Faculty Support toward the Learning Resources Center at Ricks College. Societal Factors Affecting Education. ED 247 928. Nova University, June 1984. 71 pp.

Whitlatch, Jo Bell, "Library Use Patterns among Full-and Part-Time Faculty and Students," *College & Research Libraries,* 44 (2) March 1983, 141-52.

Supplement B. Results of the Cross-Product Ratio Analysis for Selected Library, Situational, and Scholarly Activity Variables

Table 1. The cross-product relation between evaluations of the library and other variables. The first two columns specify the variables considered. The third gives the cross product ratio (XPR) and the fourth gives its logarithm, which is used to calculate significance. The fifth gives the standard error and the sixth the t-statistic. Results larger than 2 (either positive or negative) are significant at the 95 percent level and are flagged with an asterisk at the end of the line, following the page number. The page reference is to be the original printout of the cross-product ratio analysis of the ACLS survey data. No results are given for cases in which one or more of the cells of the 2 × 2 table was empty. This table appears in nine parts. (In column 1, the abbreviation in capital letters is the computer coding of the variable; the key words are spelled out below.)

Part 1 Adequacy of library collections and services and respondent disciplines

Library variables	Other variables	XPR	Log XPR	se	t	Page
LJLRES	CLASSICS	0.98	-0.03	0.23	-0.11	4
Adequacy of	ENGLISH	0.79	-0.24	0.11	-2.11	5*
journals for	HISTORY	0.86	-0.15	0.11	-1.45	6
my research	PHILO	0.92	-0.09	0.12	-0.71	7
	POLSCI	1.11	0.11	0.13	0.82	8
	LINGLNG	1.30	0.26	0.19	1.35	9
	SOCIOL	1.39	0.33	0.12	2.86	10*
	INTDSC	0.99	-0.01	0.14	-0.06	11
LJLTCH	CLASSICS	1.43	0.36	0.27	1.44	12
Adequacy of	ENGLISH	0.74	-0.30	0.12	-2.42	13*
journals for	HISTORY	1.14	0.13	0.12	1.11	14
my teaching	PHILO	0.82	-0.20	0.14	-1.39	15
	POLSCI	1.47	0.39	0.16	2.66	16*
	LINGLNG	0.89	-0.12	0.22	-0.52	17
	SOCIOL	1.14	0.13	0.14	0.98	18
	INTDSC	0.86	-0.15	0.16	-0.90	19

Part 1 Continued

Library variables	Other variables	XPR	Log XPR	se	t	Page
LJLSTU	CLASSICS	2.02	0.70	0.32	2.67	20*
Adequacy of	ENGLISH	0.81	−0.21	0.13	−1.61	21
journals for	HISTORY	1.06	0.06	0.12	0.47	22
my students	PHILO	0.98	−0.02	0.14	−0.15	23
	POLSCI	1.17	0.16	0.15	1.07	24
	LINGLNG	1.15	0.14	0.24	0.61	25
	SOCIOL	0.90	−0.10	0.13	−0.77	26
	INTDSC	0.95	−0.05	0.17	−0.29	27
LBRES	CLASSICS	1.27	0.24	0.22	1.04	28
Adequacy of	ENGLISH	0.91	−0.10	0.11	−0.88	29
books for my	HISTORY	0.66	−0.42	0.11	−3.88	30*
research	PHILO	1.10	0.10	0.13	0.77	31
	POLSCI	1.25	0.22	0.13	1.73	32
	LINGLNG	1.42	0.35	0.19	1.84	33
	SOCIOL	1.04	0.04	0.12	0.35	34
	INTDSC	1.13	0.12	0.14	0.84	35
LBTCH	CLASSICS	1.66	0.51	0.27	2.08	36*
Adequacy of	ENGLISH	1.10	0.09	0.12	0.77	37
books for	HISTORY	1.13	0.12	0.12	1.04	38
my teaching	PHILO	0.96	−0.04	0.14	−0.28	39
	POLSCI	1.08	0.08	0.14	0.54	40
	LINGLNG	0.91	−0.09	0.20	−0.44	41
	SOCIOL	0.74	−0.30	0.12	−2.40	42*
	INTDSC	0.89	−0.11	0.16	−0.69	43
LBSTU	CLASSICS	1.95	0.67	0.29	2.68	44*
Adequacy of	ENGLISH	0.97	−0.03	0.12	−0.24	45
books for	HISTORY	1.05	0.05	0.12	0.41	46
my students	PHILO	1.36	0.31	0.15	2.19	47*
	POLSCI	0.84	−0.17	0.14	−1.19	48
	LINGLNG	1.13	0.12	0.22	0.55	49
	SOCIOL	0.73	−0.31	0.13	−2.39	50*
	INTDSC	0.97	−0.03	0.17	−0.19	51
LREFLIB	CLASSICS	1.11	0.11	0.29	0.38	52
Availability	ENGLISH	0.91	−0.09	0.13	−0.69	53
of reference	HISTORY	0.73	−0.31	0.13	−2.33	54*
librarians	PHILO	1.15	0.14	0.17	0.85	55
	POLSCI	0.97	−0.04	0.16	−0.22	56
	LINGLNG	1.22	0.20	0.26	0.83	57
	SOCIOL	1.02	0.02	0.14	0.15	58
	INTDSC	1.61	0.48	0.20	2.71	59*

Part 1 Continued

Library variables	Other variables	XPR	Log XPR	se	t	Page
LDATAB	CLASSICS	1.09	0.08	0.31	0.26	60
Access to	ENGLISH	0.91	-0.10	0.13	-0.76	61
computerized	HISTORY	0.90	-0.10	0.13	-0.82	62
data bases	PHILO	0.98	-0.02	0.15	-0.10	63
	POLSCI	0.92	-0.09	0.15	-0.57	64
	LINGLNG	1.28	0.25	0.25	1.05	65
	SOCIOL	0.98	-0.02	0.13	-0.14	66
	INTDSC	1.44	0.37	0.18	2.18	67*
SONLINE	CLASSICS	0.76	-0.27	0.74	-0.38	68
Satisfaction	ENGLISH	1.62	0.48	0.24	2.02	69*
with online	HISTORY	0.43	-0.84	0.24	-3.85	70*?
searches	PHILO	1.56	0.45	0.30	1.47	71
	POLSCI	0.60	-0.52	0.26	-2.08	72*
	LINGLNG	0.82	-0.20	0.40	-0.52	73
	SOCIOL	1.21	0.19	0.20	0.97	74
	INTDSC	1.66	0.51	0.26	1.94	75

Part 2. Situational variables: Public or private university, selectivity of admissions, rank or department, sex

Library variables	Other variables	XPR	Log XPR	se	t	Page
LJLRES	PUBPRIV	1.23	0.21	0.09	2.35	77*
Adequacy of	SELECT	4.03	1.39	0.12	13.85	78*
journals for	DEPTRANK	3.30	1.19	0.22	6.96	79*
my research	SEX	1.37	0.31	0.10	3.16	80*
LJLTCH	PUBPRIV	1.09	0.08	0.10	0.82	81
Adequacy of	SELECT	3.73	1.32	0.14	11.70	82*
journals for	DEPTRANK	2.99	1.10	0.29	5.06	83*
my teaching	SEX	1.64	0.50	0.11	4.29	84*
LJLSTU	PUBPRIV	0.92	-0.09	0.10	-0.84	85
Adequacy of	SELECT	4.50	1.50	0.16	13.08	86*
journals for	DEPTRANK	3.14	1.14	0.29	5.35	87*
my students	SEX	1.71	0.54	0.11	4.59	88*
LBRES	PUBPRIV	1.09	0.08	0.09	0.91	89
Adequacy of	SELECT	3.78	1.33	0.11	12.91	90*
books for my	DEPTRANK	5.09	1.63	0.20	10.57	91*
research	SEX	1.55	0.44	0.10	4.36	92*
LBTCH	PUBPRIV	0.92	-0.09	0.10	-0.91	93
Adequacy of	SELECT	3.63	1.29	0.13	11.86	94*
books for	DEPTRANK	2.83	1.04	0.24	5.48	95*
my teaching	SEX	1.95	0.67	0.11	6.10	96*
LBSTU	PUBPRIV	0.95	-0.05	0.10	-0.51	97
Adequacy of	SELECT	3.54	1.26	0.14	11.32	98*
books for	DEPTRANK	3.48	1.25	0.25	6.71	99*
my students	SEX	1.71	0.53	0.11	4.63	100*
LREFLIB	PUBPRIV	0.70	-0.36	0.11	-3.31	101*
Availability	SELECT	2.90	1.07	0.15	8.66	102*
of reference	DEPTRANK	4.10	1.41	0.28	7.08	103*
librarians	SEX	1.44	0.36	0.12	2.90	104*
LDATAB	PUBPRIV	0.88	-0.12	0.11	-1.19	105
Access to	SELECT	2.97	1.09	0.14	9.05	106*
computerized	DEPTRANK	2.68	0.99	0.23	5.10	107*
data bases	SEX	1.15	0.14	0.12	1.14	108
SONLINE	PUBPRIV	0.73	-0.31	0.17	-1.76	109
Satisfaction	SELECT	1.58	0.46	0.21	2.23	110*
with online	DEPTRANK	1.30	0.26	0.32	0.81	111
searches	SEX	0.79	-0.23	0.19	-1.25	112

Part 3. Type of institution: Research and PhD-granting, comprehensive, liberal arts, 2-year college, other

Library variables	Other variables	XPR	Log XPR	se	t	Page
LJLRES	RESC−PHD	5.69	1.74	0.09	20.17	114*
Adequacy of	COMPR	0.33	−1.12	0.11	−10.86	115*
journals for	LIBARTS	0.36	−1.03	0.12	−8.95	116*
my research	2 YEAR	0.19	−1.66	0.27	−7.79	117*
	OTHER	0.42	−0.86	0.29	−3.14	118*
LJLTCH	RESC−PHD	4.37	1.48	0.11	14.93	119*
Adequacy of	COMPR	0.41	−0.89	0.11	−7.29	120*
journals for	LIBARTS	0.57	−0.56	0.12	−4.34	121*
my teaching	2 YEAR	0.17	−1.74	0.24	−7.15	122*
	OTHER	0.32	−1.13	0.29	−3.55	123*
LJLSTU	RESC−PHD	3.57	1.27	0.11	12.63	124*
Adequacy of	COMPR	0.47	−0.76	0.12	−6.15	125*
journals for	LIBARTS	0.65	−0.44	0.13	−3.28	126*
my students	2 YEAR	0.15	−1.87	0.24	−7.41	127*
	OTHER	0.44	−0.83	0.31	−2.42	128*
LBRES	RESC−PHD	4.78	1.57	0.10	17.98	129*
Adequacy of	COMPR	0.31	−1.16	0.12	−11.27	130*
books for my	LIBARTS	0.41	−0.89	0.13	−7.68	131*
research	2 YEAR	0.25	−1.37	0.28	−6.61	132*
	OTHER	0.50	−0.69	0.30	−2.54	133*
LBTCH	RESC−PHD	3.63	1.29	0.10	13.59	134*
Adequacy of	COMPR	0.42	−0.86	0.11	−7.56	135*
books for	LIBARTS	0.67	−0.39	0.12	−3.11	136*
my teaching	2 YEAR	0.19	−1.66	0.25	−7.09	137*
	OTHER	0.31	−1.17	0.30	−3.87	138*
LBSTU	RESC−PHD	2.47	0.90	0.10	9.22	139*
Adequacy of	COMPR	0.55	−0.60	0.11	−5.10	140*
books for	LIBARTS	0.71	−0.34	0.13	−2.61	141*
my students	2 YEAR	0.26	−1.35	0.26	−4.91	142*
	OTHER	0.45	−0.80	0.31	−2.39	143*
LREFLIB	RESC−PHD	1.37	0.32	0.11	2.95	144*
Availability	COMPR	0.82	−0.20	0.13	−1.52	145
of reference	LIBARTS	0.91	−0.10	0.14	−0.69	146
librarians	2 YEAR	0.57	−0.57	0.24	−2.09	147*
	OTHER	0.89	−0.12	0.34	−0.35	148

Part 3. Continued

Library variables	Other variables	XPR	Log XPR	se	t	Page
LDATAB	RESC-PHD	2.05	0.72	0.10	7.00	149*
Access to	COMPR	0.66	-0.42	0.12	-3.42	150*
computerized	LIBARTS	0.75	-0.29	0.13	-2.19	151*
data bases	2 YEAR	0.24	-1.41	0.25	-5.57	152*
	OTHER	1.36	0.31	0.35	0.92	153
SONLINE	RESC-PHD	0.66	-0.41	0.17	-2.39	154*
Satisfaction	COMPR	0.92	-0.09	0.20	-0.44	155
with online	LIBARTS	1.69	0.52	0.22	2.35	156*
searches	2 YEAR	2.44	0.89	0.48	1.95	157
	OTHER	1.50	0.40	0.56	0.71	158

Part 4. Academic rank: Instructor, lecturer, assistant professor, associate professor, and professor

Library variables	Other variables	XPR	Log XPR	se	t	Page
LJLRES	INSTRUCT	0.50	-0.70	0.25	-2.90	160*
Adequacy of	LECTR	2.31	0.84	0.30	3.08	161*
journals for	ASST PROF	0.51	-0.68	0.11	-6.45	162*
my research	ASSOC PROF	0.78	-0.25	0.10	-2.59	163*
	FULL PROF	2.09	0.74	0.09	8.15	164
LJLTCH	INSTRUCT	0.37	-1.00	0.24	-3.72	167*
Adequacy of	LECTR	1.13	0.12	0.33	0.37	168
journals for	ASST PROF	0.48	-0.72	0.11	-6.02	169*
my teaching	ASSOC PROF	0.83	-0.19	0.11	-1.70	170
	FULL PROF	2.45	0.90	0.11	8.87	171*
LJLSTU	INSTRUCT	0.30	-1.22	0.25	-4.38	174*
Adequacy of	LECTR	1.73	0.55	0.35	1.81	175
journals for	ASST PROF	0.45	-0.79	0.12	-6.24	176*
my students	ASSOC PROF	0.94	-0.06	0.11	-0.55	177
	FULL PROF	2.22	0.80	0.11	7.70	178*
LBRES	INSTRUCT	0.58	-0.55	0.26	-2.30	181*
Adequacy of	LECTR	1.85	0.62	0.28	2.16	182*
books for my	ASST PROF	0.50	-0.70	0.11	-6.53	183*
research	ASSOC PROF	0.80	-0.22	0.10	-2.32	184*
	FULL PROF	1.99	0.69	0.09	7.53	185*

Part 4. Continued

Library variables	Other variables	XPR	Log XPR	se	t	Page
LBTCH	INSTRUCT	0.41	-0.90	0.26	-3.35	188*
Adequacy of	LECTR	1.22	0.20	0.31	0.67	189
books for	ASST PROF	0.43	-0.84	0.11	-7.14	190*
my teaching	ASSOC PROF	0.78	-0.24	0.10	-2.33	191*
	FULL PROF	2.63	0.97	0.10	9.93	192*
LBSTU	INSTRUCT	0.41	-0.89	0.27	-3.10	195*
Adequacy of	LECTR	2.08	0.73	0.35	2.47	196*
books for	ASST PROF	0.38	-0.96	0.12	-7.93	197*
my students	ASSOC PROF	0.84	-0.17	0.11	-1.59	198
	FULL PROF	2.59	0.95	0.11	9.50	199*
LREFLIB	INSTRUCT	0.76	-0.27	0.29	-0.89	202
Availability	LECTR	1.28	0.25	0.35	0.76	203
of reference	ASST PROF	0.55	-0.60	0.13	-4.43	204*
librarians	ASSOC PROF	0.78	-0.25	0.12	-2.07	205*
	FULL PROF	2.00	0.69	0.12	6.21	206*
LDATAB	INSTRUCT	0.53	-0.64	0.29	-2.06	209*
Access to	LECTR	1.19	0.18	0.34	0.54	210
computerized	ASST PROF	0.63	-0.47	0.12	-3.64	211*
data bases	ASSOC PROF	0.80	-0.23	0.11	-1.99	212
	FULL PROF	1.86	0.62	0.11	5.85	213*
SONLINE	INSTRUCT	2.10	0.74	0.74	1.03	216
Satisfaction	LECTR	0.53	-0.64	0.70	-1.00	217
with online	ASST PROF	1.05	0.05	0.21	0.25	218
searches	ASSOC PROF	0.64	-0.45	0.19	-2.37	219*
	FULL PROF	1.43	0.36	0.18	2.00	220*

Part 5. Tenure status: Tenured, on tenure track, not on tenure track, other

Library variables	Other variables	XPR	Log XPR	se	t	Page
LJLRES	TENURE	1.47	0.39	0.09	4.29	224*
Adequacy of	TENURE TRACK	0.54	-0.61	0.11	-5.48	225*
journals for	NOTRACK	1.16	0.15	0.14	1.08	226
my research	OTHER	0.74	-0.30	0.21	-1.43	227
LJLTCH	TENURE	2.10	0.74	0.10	7.06	228*
Adequacy of	TENURE TRACK	0.52	-0.65	0.12	-5.16	229*
journals for	NOTRACK	0.67	-0.41	0.15	-2.50	230*
my teaching	OTHER	0.54	-0.61	0.24	-2.33	231*
LJLSTU	TENURE	1.90	0.64	0.10	5.97	232*
Adequacy of	TENURE TRACK	0.49	-0.71	0.12	-5.33	233*
journals for	NOTRACK	0.79	-0.23	0.16	-1.40	234
my students	OTHER	0.73	-0.31	0.24	-1.24	235
LBRES	TENURE	1.47	0.38	0.09	4.18	236*
Adequacy of	TENURE TRACK	0.55	-0.60	0.12	-5.33	237*
books for my	NOTRACK	1.06	0.06	0.14	0.41	238
research	OTHER	0.91	-0.10	0.21	-0.48	239
LBTCH	TENURE	2.11	0.75	0.10	7.38	240*
Adequacy of	TENURE TRACK	0.48	-0.73	0.12	-5.96	241*
books for	NOTRACK	0.76	-0.27	0.15	-1.74	242
my teaching	OTHER	0.51	-0.67	0.23	-2.77	243*
LBSTU	TENURE	?.24	0.81	0.10	7.73	244*
Adequacy of	TENURE TRACK	0.40	-0.91	0.12	-7.23	245*
books for	NOTRACK	0.72	-0.33	0.16	-2.02	246*
my students	OTHER	0.84	-0.18	0.25	-0.70	247
LREFLIB	TENURE	1.64	0.50	0.11	4.32	248*
Availability	TENURE TRACK	0.55	-0.60	0.13	-4.24	249*
of reference	NOTRACK	0.87	-0.14	0.17	-0.79	250
librarians	OTHER	0.90	-0.10	0.26	-0.39	251
LDATAB	TENURE	1.40	0.33	0.11	3.05	252*
Access to	TENURE TRACK	0.68	-0.38	0.13	-2.85	253*
computerized	NOTRACK	0.91	-0.09	0.17	-0.55	254
data bases	OTHER	0.78	-0.25	0.25	-0.96	255
SONLINE	TENURE	0.91	-0.09	0.18	-0.51	256
Satisfaction	TENURE TRACK	1.36	0.30	0.22	1.34	257
with online	NOTRACK	0.71	-0.34	0.28	-1.23	258
searches	OTHER	1.18	0.17	0.43	0.39	259

Part 6. Graduate degrees offered by your department: Doctorate, masters, none

Library variables	Other variables	XPR	Log XPR	se	t	Page
Adequacy of	DOCTOR	6.18	1.82	0.10	20.97	261*
journals for	MASTERS	0.55	-0.60	0.11	-5.70	262*
my research	NO	0.24	-1.43	0.10	-15.92	263*
Adequacy of	DOCTOR	5.25	1.66	0.12	16.87	264*
journals for	MASTERS	0.56	-0.58	0.12	-4.67	265*
my teaching	NO	0.31	-1.17	0.10	-11.36	266*
Adequacy of	DOCTOR	4.15	1.42	0.11	14.19	267*
journals for	MASTERS	0.61	-0.50	0.12	-4.04	268*
my students	NO	0.36	-1.01	0.10	-9.54	269*
Adequacy of	DOCTOR	4.96	1.60	0.09	18.13	270*
books for my	MASTERS	0.42	-0.87	0.12	-8.17	271*
research	NO	0.33	-1.10	0.10	-12.19	272*
Adequacy of	DOCTOR	3.97	1.38	0.10	14.53	273*
books for	MASTERS	0.53	-0.63	0.11	-5.40	274*
my teaching	NO	0.40	-0.92	0.10	-9.22	275*
Adequacy of	DOCTOR	2.99	1.10	0.10	11.23	276*
books for	MASTERS	0.59	-0.53	0.11	-4.42	277*
my students	NO	0.48	-0.72	0.10	-7.02	278*
Availability	DOCTOR	1.62	0.48	0.11	4.44	279*
of reference	MASTERS	0.70	-0.36	0.13	-2.75	280*
librarians	NO	0.79	-0.23	0.11	-2.06	281*
Access to	DOCTOR	2.06	0.72	0.11	6.98	282*
computerized	MASTERS	0.68	-0.39	0.12	-3.07	283*
data bases	NO	0.64	-0.45	0.11	-4.20	284*
Satisfaction	DOCTOR	0.82	-0.20	0.18	-1.12	285
with online	MASTERS	0.45	-0.79	0.21	-3.93	286*
searches	NO	2.29	0.83	0.18	4.57	287*

Part 7. Teaching activity: Mix of graduate and undergraduate students

Library variables	Other variables	XPR	Log XPR	se	t	Page
LJLRES	GRAD	2.33	0.85	0.22	4.14	289*
Adequacy of	MOST GRAD	2.93	1.07	0.22	5.66	290*
journals for	HALF EACH	3.64	1.29	0.14	11.03	291*
my research	MOST U	1.16	0.15	0.09	1.67	292
	ALL UNDER	0.28	-1.28	0.10	-14.03	293*
LJLTCH	GRAD	1.45	0.37	0.25	1.62	294
Adequacy of	MOST GRAD	1.88	0.63	0.24	3.11	295*
journals for	HALF EACH	3.34	1.21	0.17	9.37	296*
my teaching	MOST U	1.15	0.14	0.10	1.35	297
	ALL UNDER	0.38	-0.96	0.10	-9.25	298*
LJLSTU	GRAD	1.41	0.35	0.26	1.43	299
Adequacy of	MOST GRAD	1.64	0.50	0.24	2.36	300*
journals for	HALF EACH	2.89	1.06	0.17	7.98	301*
my students	MOST U	1.32	0.28	0.11	2.63	302*
	ALL UNDER	0.37	-0.99	0.10	-9.24	303*
LBRES	GRAD	2.20	0.79	0.22	3.67	304*
Adequacy of	MOST GRAD	2.94	1.08	0.20	5.58	305*
books for my	HALF EACH	3.26	1.18	0.12	9.95	306*
research	MOST U	0.92	-0.08	0.09	-0.90	307
	ALL UNDER	0.34	-1.07	0.10	-11.73	308*
LBTCH	GRAD	1.52	0.42	0.25	1.83	309
Adequacy of	MOST GRAD	1.97	0.68	0.23	3.43	310*
books for	HALF EACH	2.25	0.81	0.14	6.54	311*
my teaching	MOST U	1.14	0.13	0.10	1.33	312
	ALL UNDER	0.44	-0.81	0.10	-8.17	313*
LBSTU	GRAD	1.57	0.45	0.27	1.86	314
Adequacy of	MOST GRAD	1.65	0.50	0.23	2.45	315*
books for	HALF EACH	1.83	0.60	0.14	4.69	316*
my students	MOST U	1.09	0.09	0.10	0.86	317
	ALL UNDER	0.53	-0.63	0.10	-6.11	318*
LREFLIB	GRAD	1.88	0.63	0.32	2.42	319*
Availability	MOST GRAD	2.28	0.82	0.29	3.63	320*
of reference	HALF EACH	1.41	0.34	0.16	2.34	321*
librarians	MOST U	0.86	-0.15	0.11	-1.35	322
	ALL UNDER	0.75	-0.29	0.11	-2.55	323*

Part 7. Continued

Library variables	Other variables	XPR	Log XPR	se	t	Page
LDATAB	GRAD	2.00	0.69	0.28	2.94	324*
Access to	MOST GRAD	1.44	0.36	0.23	1.68	325
computeized	HALF EACH	1.61	0.48	0.15	3.48	326*
data bases	MOST U	1.00	-0.00	0.11	-0.02	327
	ALL UNDER	0.61	-0.49	0.11	-4.50	328*
SONLINE	GRAD	2.46	0.90	0.37	2.52	329*
Satisfaction	MOST GRAD	1.11	0.10	0.32	0.32	330
with online	HALF EACH	0.86	-0.15	0.24	-0.62	331
searches	MOST U	0.61	-0.49	0.19	-2.70	332*
	ALL UNDER	1.36	0.31	0.19	1.64	333

Part 8. Overall satisfaction, from very satisfied to very unsatisfied

Library variables	Other variables	XPR	Log XPR	se	t	Page
LJLRES	VERY	2.40	0.87	0.09	9.95	335*
Adequacy of	MILDLY	0.90	-0.10	0.09	-1.14	336
journals for	NEUTRAL	0.75	-0.29	0.22	-1.30	337
my research	MILD UNSAT	0.39	-0.93	0.13	-7.27	338*
	VERY UNSAT	0.38	-0.98	0.17	-6.16	339*
LJLTCH	VERY	2.84	1.04	0.11	10.53	341*
Adequacy of	MILDLY	1.02	0.02	0.11	0.17	342
journals for	NEUTRAL	0.41	-0.90	0.24	-3.42	343*
my teaching	MILD UNSAT	0.42	-0.88	0.14	-5.79	344*
	VERY UNSAT	0.28	-1.28	0.17	-7.13	345*
LJLSTU	VERY	2.88	1.06	0.11	10.42	347*
Adequacy of	MILDLY	0.90	-0.10	0.11	-0.97	348
journals for	NEUTRAL	0.53	-0.63	0.25	-2.30	349*
my students	MILD UNSAT	0.47	-0.75	0.14	-4.84	350*
	VERY UNSAT	0.28	-1.26	0.17	-6.76	351*
LBRES	VERY	2.74	1.01	0.09	11.36	353*
Adequacy of	MILDLY	0.76	-0.28	0.10	-2.97	354*
books for my	NEUTRAL	0.75	-0.29	0.24	-1.22	355
research	MILD UNSAT	0.40	-0.93	0.15	-7.23	356*
	VERY UNSAT	0.34	-1.09	0.19	-6.99	357*

Part 8. Continued

Library variables	Other variables	XPR	Log XPR	se	t	Page
LBTCH	VERY	3.27	1.18	0.10	12.42	359*
Adequacy of	MILDLY	0.90	-0.11	0.10	-1.08	360
books for	NEUTRAL	0.57	-0.57	0.24	-2.25	361*
my teaching	MILD UNSAT	0.37	-0.99	0.14	-7.03	362*
	VERY UNSAT	0.24	-1.42	0.17	-8.18	363*
LBSTU	VERY	3.04	1.11	0.11	11.29	365*
Adequacy of	MILDLY	0.88	-0.13	0.10	-1.19	366
books for	NEUTRAL	0.60	-0.51	0.26	-1.86	367
my students	MILD UNSAT	0.44	-0.81	0.14	-5.57	368*
	VERY UNSAT	0.25	-1.38	0.17	-7.79	369*
LREFLIB	VERY	3.31	1.20	0.12	11.02	371*
Availability	MILDLY	0.86	-0.15	0.11	-1.25	372
of reference	NEUTRAL	0.36	-1.03	0.26	-3.39	373*
librarians	MILD UNSAT	0.45	-0.80	0.15	-4.95	374*
	VERY UNSAT	0.32	-1.13	0.18	-5.57	375*
LDATAB	VERY	2.91	1.07	0.11	10.31	377*
Access to	MILDLY	0.83	-0.19	0.11	-1.72	378
computerized	NEUTRAL	0.42	-0.88	0.27	-3.05	379*
data bases	MILD UNSAT	0.45	-0.79	0.14	-5.21	380*
	VERY UNSAT	0.34	-1.09	0.19	-5.43	381*
SONLINE	VERY	2.10	0.74	0.18	4.28	383*
Satisfaction	MILDLY	0.84	-0.18	0.19	-0.94	384
with online	NEUTRAL	0.53	-0.63	0.43	-1.56	385
searches	MILD UNSAT	0.46	-0.77	0.28	-3.04	386*
	VERY UNSAT	0.59	-0.53	0.34	-1.63	387

Part 9. External scholarly activity: Number of certificates, scholarly books, chapters, articles, conference papers, short story novel or poems published

Library variables	Other variables	XPR	Log XPR	se	t	Page
LJLRES Adequacy of journals for my research	NOSOC	0.98	-0.02	0.10	-0.24	390
	NOTXT	0.42	-0.87	0.13	-7.14	394*
	NOAUTH	0.54	-0.62	0.15	-4.30	395*
	NOCHAP	0.54	-0.61	0.13	-4.72	396*
	NOART	0.50	-0.70	0.11	-6.49	397*
	NOPAPR	0.63	-0.46	0.09	-5.03	398*
	NOSS	1.39	0.33	0.14	2.33	399*
LJLTCH Adequacy of journals for my teaching	NOSOC	0.95	-0.06	0.12	-0.47	401
	NOTXT	0.46	-0.77	0.16	-5.69	405*
	NOAUTH	0.50	-0.69	0.18	-3.88	406*
	NOCHAP	0.65	-0.43	0.16	-2.79	407*
	NOART	0.50	-0.70	0.13	-5.53	408*
	NOPAPR	0.66	-0.42	0.10	-3.98	409*
	NOSS	1.68	0.52	0.15	3.19	410*
LJLSTU Adequacy of journals for my students	NOSOC	0.94	-0.06	0.12	-0.53	412
	NOTXT	0.52	-0.66	0.16	-4.79	416*
	NOAUTH	0.53	-0.64	0.18	-3.60	417*
	NOCHAP	0.82	-0.20	0.16	-1.27	418
	NOART	0.51	-0.68	0.13	-5.22	419*
	NOPAPR	0.61	-0.50	0.11	-4.71	420*
	NOSS	1.70	0.53	0.16	3.19	421*
LBRES Adequacy of books for my research	NOSOC	0.84	-0.18	0.10	-1.71	423
	NOTXT	0.38	-0.97	0.12	-7.86	427*
	NOAUTH	0.57	-0.56	0.14	-4.00	428*
	NOCHAP	0.54	-0.62	0.13	-4.92	429*
	NOART	0.47	-0.75	0.11	-7.05	430*
	NOPAPR	0.67	-0.41	0.09	-4.36	431*
	NOSS	1.05	0.05	0.14	0.35	432
LBTCH Adequacy of books for my teaching	NOSOC	0.91	-0.10	0.11	-0.86	434
	NOTXT	0.49	-0.71	0.14	-5.54	438*
	NOAUTH	0.58	-0.54	0.17	-3.33	439*
	NOCHAP	0.82	-0.20	0.14	-1.41	440
	NOART	0.58	-0.55	0.12	-4.60	441*
	NOPAPR	0.74	-0.29	0.10	-2.94	442*
	NOSS	1.43	0.36	0.15	2.33	443*

Part 9. Continued

Library variables	Other variables	XPR	Log XPR	se	t	Page
LBSTU Adequacy of books for my students	NOSOC	0.83	-0.19	0.12	-1.65	445
	NOTXT	0.46	-0.78	0.15	-5.87	449*
	NOAUTH	0.61	-0.49	0.17	-2.90	450*
	NOCHAP	0.98	-0.02	0.15	-0.11	451
	NOART	0.62	-0.49	0.12	-3.95	452*
	NOPAPR	0.70	-0.36	0.10	-3.45	453*
	NOSS	1.57	0.45	0.15	2.83	454*
LREFLIB Availability of reference librarians	NOSOC	0.99	-0.01	0.13	-0.11	456
	NOTXT	0.52	-0.65	0.17	-4.46	460*
	NOAUTH	0.77	-0.27	0.18	-1.46	461
	NOCHAP	0.82	-0.19	0.16	-1.22	462
	NOART	0.71	-0.35	0.13	-2.64	463*
	NOPAPR	0.70	-0.36	0.11	-3.15	464*
	NOSS	1.19	0.17	0.17	1.00	465
LDATAB Access to computeized data bases	NOSOC	0.96	-0.04	0.12	-0.35	467
	NOTXT	0.53	-0.64	0.15	-4.61	471*
	NOAUTH	0.69	-0.37	0.18	-2.07	472*
	NOCHAP	0.85	-0.16	0.16	-1.01	473
	NOART	0.76	-0.27	0.13	-2.12	474*
	NOPAPR	0.71	-0.35	0.11	-3.14	475*
	NOSS	0.81	-0.21	0.17	-1.24	476
SONLINE Satisfaction with online searches	NOSOC	0.97	-0.03	0.19	-0.18	478
	NOTXT	0.84	-0.17	0.24	-0.69	482
	NOAUTH	0.81	-0.21	0.27	-0.76	483
	NOCHAP	1.34	0.29	0.25	1.19	484
	NOART	0.95	-0.05	0.22	-0.24	485
	NOPAPR	0.93	-0.08	0.19	-0.41	486
	NOSS	0.56	-0.57	0.27	-2.09	487*